The distinctive, classical building of Ny Carlsberg Glyptotek (page 44)

with the famous Trundholm Sun Chariot

The equestrian statue of Christian IX at Christiansborg (page 38), seat of the Danish Parliament

The colourful harbour of Nyhavn (page 46) is lined with bars and restaurants

On duty at Amalienborg Slot (page 49), home of the royal family

The night-time illuminations at the popular Tivoli Gardens (page 26)

The 17th-century palace, Rosenborg Slot (page 60), houses the crown jewels

CONTENTS

A ➤ *in the text denotes a highly recommended sight*

Berlitz®
Copenhagen

Written *by* Norman Renouf
Photography *by* Rudy Hemmingsen
Updated *by* Jack Jackson
Edited *by* Jane Hutchings
Series Editor: Tony Halliday

Berlitz® POCKET GUIDE

Copenhagen

Fifth Edition 2006
Updated 2007

PHOTOGRAPHY CREDITS
All photography by Rudy Hemmingsen, except pages 3 and 18 (akg-images), page 17 (Jon Davison) and pages 20 and 102 (Jeroen Snidjers)
Cover picture by Superstock/Steve Vidler

CONTACTING THE EDITORS
Every effort has been made to provide accurate information in this publication, but changes are inevitable. The publisher cannot be responsible for any resulting loss, inconvenience or injury. We would appreciate it if readers would call our attention to any errors or outdated information by contacting Berlitz Publishing, PO Box 7910, London SE1 1WE, England.
Fax: (44) 20 7403 0290;
e-mail: berlitz@apaguide.co.uk
www.berlitzpublishing.com

Visit Denmark's Viking heritage at nearby Roskilde (page 79)

Vor Frelsers Kirke (page 64) with its spiralling staircase and copper-clad tower

The diminutive statue of The Little Mermaid (page 51) reclining on rocks in Langelinie

Fact Sheets

INTRODUCTION

Copenhagen (København in Danish), the capital of Denmark, is located on the eastern side of Zealand, the largest of Denmark's 406 islands, with only the Øresund (Strait) separating it from Sweden. It was founded by Bishop Absalon in 1167, and these days is home, including its greater metropolitan area, to about 1,500,000 of the country's estimated 5.5 million people. Incidentally, with a land area of just 43,000 sq km (16,630 sq miles), Denmark is the smallest yet most densely populated nation in northern Europe. In Denmark there are over six times as many people per square kilometre as in neighbouring Sweden.

> **Denmark has the oldest royal dynasty in Europe, now headed by Queen Margrethe II – the nation's first reigning queen – and her French-born husband, Prince Henrik.**

Connected by the south of Jutland to Germany, Denmark is the only Scandinavian country physically joined to the European mainland and, as such, it is the bridge between Scandinavia and the rest of the continent. Consequently, Denmark shares many of the characteristics of its Nordic neighbours: liberal welfare benefits coupled with a high standard of living, and a style of government that aims at consensus and the avoidance of petty bureaucracy. Yet Denmark is also more 'European' and accessible than the rest of Scandinavia, and its appeal is universal.

Copenhagen, with its strategic location at the mouth of the Baltic Sea, has become an important crossroads. The capital city is the political centre of Denmark, the seat of royalty

Equestrian statue of Frederik V at Amalienborg

and also the cultural centre of the country. As such, it not only offers many historical elements, chief of which are the Christiansborg complex, Rosenborg Slot and the Amalienborg palaces, a multitude of museums – more than 60 at the last count – and theatres. It has also claimed for itself a reputation as one of northern Europe's jazz capitals. Copenhagen is renowned for its shops. Strøget – said to be the longest pedestrianised street in the world – has the most eclectic array of stores to be found anywhere. Of course, most of these offer products by celebrated Danish – and Scandinavian – designers, combining functionality and aesthetics.

The People

Copenhagen's attractions are much wider than just history, culture and shopping; one of its great appeals is the character of the Danes themselves. The people are gregarious, loqua-

Canalside nightlife along Nyhavn

cious and, at one and the same time, charming and sarcastic. Besides all of this they simply love enjoying life, especially when it comes to the combination of family, friends, food and, of course, copious amounts of alcohol. In fact, there is a word, almost unpronounce-able in English, *hygge*, that loosely translated means a combination of warmth, well-being and intimacy. This can be felt at all times in every part of Copen-

Strolling in Kongens Have

hagen, but is more obvious, especially on public holidays and warm sunny days, in the many parks, such as Rosenborg Have and Ørstedsparken, and popular meeting places like Rådhuspladsen and Nyhavn that make this such an attractive city. Nowhere is it more evident than in that world-famous crown jewel of the city, Tivoli Gardens.

Fantasy and Culture

A strong sense of fantasy and colour fills the atmosphere in Copenhagen. Postmen wear bright red jackets and ride yellow bicycles, chimney-sweeps pass by wearing black top hats and buses drive along with red and white Danish flags fluttering on both sides of the cab.

Although Copenhagen is a major capital city, it is very compact, with a well-preserved old-town area of winding cobbled streets, stuccoed houses and a network of canals, and almost everything is easily accessible by foot. Despite the fact that the reliable public transport system is superb, walking around Copenhagen is, in reality, the best way to discover this city's inestimable charms.

Long before the phrase was immortalised in song by Danny Kaye, Copenhagen was known to be 'wonderful, wonderful' – a clean, green city full of gaiety, culture and charm, with a tradition of tolerance and humour.

Out and About

But that's not all. Within a very short distance of Copenhagen, and easily accessible on daytrips, are three major places of interest: Roskilde with its superb cathedral and Viking Ship Museum; Hillerød's beautiful Frederiksborg Castle; and Helsingør's dramatic Kronborg Castle used by Shakespeare in his great drama, *Hamlet*. Beyond these, Sweden lies just across the Øresund. Helsingborg is directly opposite Helsingør, and is reached in less than half an hour on one of the numerous ferries that ply the sound. Malmø can be reached by road or rail over the Øresund Bridge in just 35 minutes.

Wooden boats are still being built at Roskilde using old skills

Other destinations worthy of consideration are Dragør, a small fishing village near the airport, and the Louisiana Museum of Modern Art at Humlebæk, in a sublime setting on the coast north of Copenhagen.

A BRIEF HISTORY

Well before the Vikings organised themselves into an extraordinary nation of seafarers, Denmark was inhabited by hunting peoples. Prehistoric relics of all kinds – some dating back to 50,000BC – are displayed in Copenhagen's museums. The oldest surviving costumes in Europe have been found in this area, as have various musical instruments, including more than 30 examples of the Danish lur, which emits hoarse notes that seem strangely out of keeping with the long, graceful S-shaped stem characteristic of the instrument.

Viking Age

The first written records of the Vikings appear around AD800, at which time Viking raids on neighbouring European countries were becoming notorious. At their peak, these fearless warriors had reached Newfoundland, were rounding the North Cape and making sallies to Britain, Holland, France, Spain, the Mediterranean. Examples of their boats are on display at the Roskilde Viking Ship Museum *(see page 80)*.

Danish raids upon England gathered in strength during the late 10th century and the first years of the 11th century, culminating in an attempt at conquest. Canute (Knud) the Great, after meeting considerable resistance, finally became King of England in 1016. The union was to last until 1042.

Christianity had been introduced into Denmark in 826 by a Benedictine monk, and received the royal seal of

For a visual account of the city's colourful past and its better-known characters, call into Københavns Bymuseum (Vesterbrogade 59; open Thur–Mon 10am–4pm, Wed 10am–9pm; tel: 33 21 07 72; <www.bymuseum.dk>; admission fee).

approval in 961 when King Harald (Bluetooth) was converted by a monk named Poppo, who convinced him by seizing red-hot irons in his bare hands. A large runic stone set up by Harald at Jelling in East Jutland records that he had 'won for himself all Denmark and Norway and made the Danes Christians'.

Medieval Times

In 1157, Valdemar I (the Great) came to the throne. He leaned heavily on the influence of Bishop Absalon of Roskilde, and this proved a partnership of critical importance to Copenhagen, then just a little fishing village called Havn. With its fine harbour on the Strait (Øresund in Danish) – the waterway between Denmark and Sweden, which forms the main entrance to the Baltic – the village found itself well-placed on what was becoming one of the main trading routes of medieval Europe.

War-hero as well as statesman, Bishop Absalon fortified Havn by constructing a castle on its small harbour island of Slotsholmen in 1167; this is now acknowledged to be the founding date of the modern city. The name Havn became Køpmannæhafn ('merchants' harbour') in 1170, and eventually København. Today, Slotsholmen lies at the heart of the city. The impressive Christiansborg parliament buildings

Bishop Absalon

Absalon (1128–1201), Bishop of Roskilde, Archbishop of Lund and founder of Copenhagen, was also a statesman, a warrior – who successfully waged war against the terrorising Wends – and a literary patron. His foster brother, Valdemar I, granted him the fishing village of Havn where Absalon built a stronghold on the site now occupied by Christiansborg *(see page 38)*. The bishop commissioned his secretary, Saxo, to produce *Gesta Danorum*, an estimable history of Denmark.

The equestrian statue of Bishop Absalon on Højbro Plads

now occupy the site, but you can see some intriguing remnants of Absalon's castle in their cellars *(see page 40)*.

In the 12th century Denmark sorely overextended itself in all directions, and for this it paid dearly in the 13th and 14th centuries. It had interfered in the government of Schleswig and Holstein as well as troubling the growing trade of the north German Hanseatic ports. The Germans marched into Jutland. The Danish aristocracy seized the opportunity to curb the powers of its monarchy, and in 1282 King Erik V was forced to sign a Great Charter under which he would rule together with the nobles in the Council of the Danish Realm.

Nevertheless, Valdemar IV Atterdag (*c.*1320–75), probably the greatest of medieval Danish kings, led the country back onto a path of conquests and into new conflict with its Nordic neighbours, setting a pattern that was to last, intermittently, for centuries. Denmark's hand was greatly strengthened when Valdemar's daughter Margrete married Håkon VI, King of

Norway and Sweden. After his death, Margrete succeeded through the Treaty of Kalmar in 1397 in unifying the three Nordic powers under her nephew Erik VII of Pomerania. Indomitable Margrete ruled in his name, but was struck down by the plague at the peak of her power in 1412.

During the later, true reign of Erik VII (1412–39), Copenhagen was enlarged. The city then became the official Danish capital under Christopher III of Bavaria in the 1440s; when a university was founded by Christian I in 1479, it also became the country's cultural centre. By this time, the city's population had increased to about 10,000; Schleswig-Holstein was again under Danish rule, and a castle was being built at Helsingør (the Elsinore of Shakespeare's *Hamlet*) to enforce the payment of tolls on the Øresund. Control of the Øresund was vital to Denmark's strategic strength at the crossroads of the northern seas. Dues were exacted from each ship passing through the 3-km (2-mile) wide channel between Helsingør on Zealand and Helsingborg in Sweden.

By then Denmark stood in a very strong position. New towns and villages had mushroomed. The scene was set for a turbulent period of 200 years marked by civil war against the nobles, the advent of the Lutheran movement in Denmark, and more wars with Sweden. In 1523 the Swedes revolted after the infamous 'Stockholm Bloodbath', causing the dissolution of the Kalmar Union and the independence of Sweden, although Denmark and Norway remained united.

The Reformation

In the 16th century, with the unprecedented spread of ideas, the latent, deep-seated discontent regarding abuses within the Catholic Church began to be brought out into the open. In Denmark, Catholic bishops had long been putting their wealth to political and military uses, and it was left to Christian III (1534–59) to break their stranglehold. He declared himself supreme authority of a state church based on Lutheranism in 1536, which had made deep inroads since arriving from Germany. The bishops were imprisoned until they 'consented'.

Meanwhile, the wars with Sweden lurched on disastrously. By the latter half of the 17th century Denmark had been forced to relinquish her remaining Swedish possessions, and to cede the east bank of the Øresund to Sweden. This crucial waterway was now split down the middle, jointly controlled by the two Scandinavian powers, as it still is today.

As Denmark licked its many 17th-century war wounds, the city of Copenhagen was given two great consolations. It was declared a free city in 1660 as an acknowledgement of its bravery during a two-year blockade by Sweden, and this meant that all residents were accorded the same privileges as the nobles. Secondly, under Christian IV it had experienced a wave of new culture and fine building. The 'Great Builder', as he was known, had effectively doubled the size of the city during the earlier part of the century. He was responsible for the existence of so many of the green copper roofs that make the Copenhagen skyline uniquely photogenic, notably the Round Tower, the Stock Exchange and Rosenborg Castle.

Christian IV's Rosenborg Castle

Absolute Power

As a result of the Swedish wars, Denmark was bankrupted and its country laid waste, and both political and social upheavals became inevitable.

In 1660, King Frederik III matched the mood of the moment and proclaimed himself absolute monarch, thereby depriving all the nobles of the Council of the Danish Realm of the powers they had enjoyed since 1282. Frederik's absolute rule presided over a period of national unity, with a tightly controlled, well-organised central bureaucracy.

The early absolutist kings still waged several costly wars, mainly against the Swedish. Copenhagen suffered a terrible plague in 1711–12 which killed 22,000 people – nearly a third of its inhabitants – as well as two devastating fires in 1728 and 1795.

The 18th century was highlighted by major social change. Serfdom was abolished in 1788 (note the Freedom Pillar in Vesterbrogade, opposite the Central Station) and peasants threw off the yoke of the medieval landlord and began to work for themselves. This emancipation gave the Danish countryside its present character of a landscape dotted with farms, and was of enormous influence in the shaping of modern Denmark.

Napoleon and the 19th Century

Denmark found itself reluctantly involved in the revolutionary wars of late-18th-century Europe. By maintaining their participation with Russia, Sweden and Prussia in the League of Armed Neutrality – intended to thwart Great Britain's claim to the right of searching all vessels at sea – Denmark brought down upon itself the ire of the British. In 1801, a fleet under admirals Nelson and Parker sailed into the bay of Copenhagen. During the ensuing battle, Nelson, so legend has it, raised a telescope to his blind eye so as to be able to deny having been aware of a signal to break off the engagement.

Afraid that Napoleon would take over the Dano-Norwegian fleet, Britain subsequently demanded its instant surrender. When the Danes refused to acquiesce, Copenhagen was blockaded and in 1807 subjected to a three-day bombardment by the British Navy. Denmark had no choice but to hand over what was left of its fleet to the British, only to be forced immediately afterwards to agree to an alliance with Napoleon, who was by then marching fast into Jutland.

When Napoleon was finally brought to his knees, Denmark emerged completely isolated on account of this alliance. Norway was handed over to Sweden in 1814 in payment of war debts and the formerly vast Danish territories overseas were reduced to Greenland, Iceland, the Faroes and the Virgin Islands. Fifty years later Denmark was further reduced by the loss of the duchies of Schleswig and Holstein – a third of its

The combined Danish and French fleet arrives, ready to fight, in a 19th-century painting by marine artist Carl Neumann

N.F.S. Grundtvig, priest, writer and pioneering educationalist

home territory and two-fifths of its population – to Bismarck's Prussia. Following a spate of civil turmoil in Denmark provoked by the 1848 revolution in France, Frederik VII was forced to relinquish his absolute rule and hand over the reigns of power to the National Liberal Party.

A liberal constitution was drawn up with wide suffrage, and the Danish 'Golden Age' was all set to begin. Hans Christian Andersen (1805–75), the writer from Odense, was strolling the city streets, reading his fairytales to groups of admirers.

In the city, factories and housing blocks for workers sprang up, so that by the late 19th century Copenhagen was a thriving industrial centre. Meanwhile, changes were beginning to take place in the countryside. The theologian and politician N.F.S. Grundtvig (1783–1872), established his system of popular adult high schools in 1844 to improve the peasant's lot.

The 20th Century

In 1901 an important landmark was reached in Danish constitutional history when a government based only on a majority in the lower chamber of parliament (Folketing) was appointed. The march of the common people brought them not only into the cities and urban areas, but also right into the political struggle. In 1915, the Liberal Democrats, Social Democrats an Radical Liberals jointly forced the abolition of electoral privileges in the upper chamber (Landstinget) and initiated a system of proportional representation for both chambers. At the same time, the vote was at last given to women and servants.

The new Danish society was put under severe strain in the process of adopting the compromises necessary to maintain neutrality during World War I. After the war north Schleswig voted itself back into Denmark, establishing the shape of today's border. Industrial unrest and economic depression between the two world wars failed to halt the progress of Denmark. In the design of consumer goods – furniture, cutlery, glass, pewter, silver and textiles – Denmark set new standards, combining utility with beauty, to the point where 'Danish design' became synonymous with good, functional, yet aesthetically pleasing articles.

When World War II broke out in 1939 the Scandinavian nations issued their declarations of neutrality. Nevertheless, on 9 April 1940 Denmark was invaded by Germany. After a token struggle, the country's defences collapsed and the nation fell under German control. However, the anti-Nazi sentiments of the vast majority of Danes were expressed by cold-shoulder treatment, and eventually acted upon through outright resistance. The Danes managed by various means to smuggle 7,000 of Denmark's 7,500 Jews out of the country and into neighbouring Sweden.

The wartime king, Christian X, became the country's folk-hero. In 1943, the government resigned – it could no longer yield to German demands without losing the support of the population. The resistance was so organised that Denmark was already a full member of the Allied forces by the time the war came to an end in 1945. So began a new era of massive Danish reconstruction, resulting in the present modern-day society – one of the world's most successful attempts at a welfare state.

Politically, Denmark abandoned neutrality when it became a member of NATO in 1949. Economically, it was a founding member of the European Free Trade Association (EFTA), and joined the European Economic Community (subsequently the European Union) with the UK and Ireland in 1972.

Modern Denmark

Denmark today is one of the most prosperous countries in Europe, and its population of around 5.5 million enjoys an extremely high standard of living. At the World Summit in Copenhagen in 1995, Denmark was one of the only countries to forgive a sizeable amount of Third-World debt.

The fact that Denmark's influence is felt beyond its frontiers testifies to its important role in the future of a cohesive Europe. However, in 2000 the people of Denmark voted in a referendum not to adopt the euro as their currency. In the 2001 elections the right-wing parties, on a platform of anti-immigration and law and order, increased their vote to form a coalition government. In February 2005 they won a second term in office.

Later in 2005, Danish foreign affairs took a turn for the worse, when a national newspaper published 12 cartoons of the

The Danish flag

Prophet Muhammad, causing protests and boycots, particularly in the Muslim world. A debate raged in Denmark and abroad over the meaning of freedom of speech and when something becomes blasphemous. The Danish Prime Minister Anders Fogh Rasmussen described the controversy as Denmark's worst international crisis since World War II.

Historical Landmarks

1167 King Valdemar the Great gives Bishop Absalon of Roskilde land by the Øresund, which includes the fishing and trading settlement of Havn. Absalon builds a castle on the island of Holmen.

1254 The village of Køpmannæhafn receives a municipal charter. The Hanseatic League uses the port as a staging post for Baltic trade.

1376 Absalon's castle is replaced by København Slot.

1397–1534 Denmark sets up the Kalmar Union with Norway and Sweden.

1417 Erik VII makes Copenhagen his capital. Ships on the Øresund have to pay tolls from 1425. Trade flourishes; the population rises to 10,000.

1479 The university is founded by Christian I.

1588–1648 Christian IV enlarges the town and harbour and commissions grand Renaissance-style buildings, including Rosenborg Slot and Børsen. Thirty Years War destroys Denmark's prosperity.

1660 Copenhagen is declared a free city.

1711–12 Plague kills one third of Copenhagen's inhabitants.

1732 Christian VI replaces København Slot with Christiansborg Palace.

Early 1800s The British fleet under Nelson demands the surrender of the Danish fleet in Napoleonic Wars. Subsequent bombardment ruins the city.

Late 1800s Denmark's 'Golden Age' of arts and science. Tivoli Gardens open; the first railway line links Copenhagen with Roskilde; city ramparts are demolished; industrialisation draws in country people.

1914–18 Denmark remains neutral during World War I.

1918 New Christiansborg Palace becomes the seat of Danish parliament.

1924 Social Democrats win power; a welfare state is established.

1940–5 Denmark is occupied by German forces.

1950–70 Modern satellite towns spring up around Copenhagen.

1971 Young people establish the Free State of Christiania.

1972 Margrethe II crowned. Denmark joins EEC (today's European Union).

2000 Øresund Bridge opens between Denmark and Sweden.

2001 Election of right-wing government; policy to restrict immigration.

2005–6 'Muhammad drawings' in the Jyllands-Posten newspaper push the government into a major diplomatic crisis.

GETTING AROUND

You will have no problem finding your way around this delightfully compact city. Most of the important sights and museums are contained within the central section and bounded by the former medieval ramparts, so exploring Copenhagen on foot is a real pleasure. There is also the network of canals that offer many opportunities for waterside walks and gentle excursions afloat. And if you want a change of pace from sightseeing or shopping, the abundance of leafy parks and attractive gardens provides a very welcome and pleasant retreat.

> Museum opening times and admission fees are subject to change. It is advisable to check the listing in the free guide, *Copenhagen This Week*. The Copenhagen Card *(see page 125)* offers free or discounted entry.

AROUND RÅDHUSPLADSEN

Every city has a social gathering point, but Copenhagen has more than one. Without a doubt, the centrally located **Rådhuspladsen** (City Hall Square) is the most popular and, consequently, most of the suggested planned walks start from here. It is also the stopping point for the main bus routes and is near Central Station, where trains depart for the suburbs and beyond.

It is in this large open square, with a café and ubiquitous hot-dog stands *(pølsevogn)* – where tasty Danish sausages are served in a variety of inexpensive forms – that you can take the opportunity to observe Danish life.

Hans Christian Andersen, author and poet

City Hall

The dominant building in Rådhuspladsen is the red-brick **Rådhus** (City Hall) with its 105-m (345-ft) tower. Built between 1892 and 1905, it is reached via broad steps which play host to impromptu concerts. Its main doorway is crowned by a statue of Bishop Absalon, the founder of the city *(see page 12)*, in copper and 22-carat gilt. On the roof above you'll see six bronze figures of night watchmen dating from various periods of the city's history. Each section of the Rådhus bears a different style and imprint, but they come together architecturally very much like a patchwork quilt. The main hall and banqueting room are impressive with their statuary and coats-of-arms – especially the view of the 44-m (145-ft) long hall from the first-floor colonnade (guided tours Mon–Fri 3pm, Sat 10am and 11am; tel: 33 66 25 82; admission fee; <www.kk.dk>).

If you are feeling energetic, there are also guided tours of **City Hall Tower** and its 300 steps (June–Sept Mon–Fri 10am, noon, 2pm; Sat noon; Oct–May Mon–Sat noon; admission fee). On a clear day you can see north along the coast and across the Øresund to Sweden. In the foyer of City Hall a sign points to **Jens Olsen's World Clock** (open Mon–Fri 10am–4pm, Sat 10am–1pm; admission fee). This intriguing astronomical clock shows time around the world, the positions of the planets and the Gregorian calendar.

Lur Players on Rådhuspladsen

Lurs and Legends

To your right as you leave the City Hall, on Vester Voldgade, is a statue that

Rådhuspladsen, focal point of city life

brings a smile to every Dane's face, the **Lur Players**. Legend
has it that the two men on top will sound a note on their
instruments if a virgin passes by – although they've been
standing on the column since 1914 and led a life of silence.
On the opposite corner of the square is the dramatic copper
Bull-and-Dragon Fountain (1923), depicting a fierce,
watery battle between the two beasts. Not far away sits a
bronze version of Denmark's favourite son, storyteller Hans
Christian Andersen, near the boulevard that bears his name.
It is on this busy road that you'll notice a very prominent
feature of Danish life – the ubiquitous bicycle.

The road to the northwest of Rådhuspladsen is Vester-
brogade, which leads to Central Station, the **Tourist Infor-
mation Office** *(see page 125)* and the entrance to Tivoli
Gardens. The monument on Versterbrogade is the Freedom
Pillar (1797), erected to commemorate the end of serfdom in
Denmark in 1788. It was designed by Nikolaj Abildgård.

ardens

Hans Christian Andersens Boulevard from Rådhus-
sen is Copenhagen's most famous attraction, **Tivoli
ardens** (main entrance Vesterbrogade 3; open daily mid-
Apr–mid-June and mid-Aug–mid-Sept Sun–Wed 11am–
11pm, Thur and Sat till midnight, Fri till 1am; mid-Jun–mid-
Aug Sun–Thur 11am–midnight, Fri–Sat 11am–1am; mid-
Nov–mid-Dec Mon–Thur 11am–10pm, Fri 11am–11pm, Sat–
Sun 10am–11pm; tel: 33 15 10 01; admission fee; <www.
tivoli.dk>).

Opened in 1843, this old-time pleasure park offers an
eclectic combination of theatrical performances, concerts,
fun fair and amusements, fireworks displays and restaurants,
all set in beautiful gardens in the heart of the city. But this is
more than just a pleasure park: new arrivals are welcomed
by neatly uniformed attendants dressed in old-fashioned out-

Night-time illuminations at Tivoli's pagoda

fits who embody a sense of tradition and dignity – special qualities of Tivoli. At the Pantomime Theatre, for instance (to the left of the main entrance), shows are accompanied not by tape recordings, but by a small orchestra, which plays on between performances in the nearby Promenade Pavilion. Performances at the theatre have included Italian *commedia dell'arte*, and a new adaptation of the ballet *Thumbelina*, with costumes by Queen Margrethe herself. (Entrance is included in your admission to the park.)

Tivoli throws open its doors for the festive season in the run-up to Christmas each year. The lake is frozen for skating and stalls offer tempting seasonal wares.

Exotic Wonderland

With its lake and lawns, water features and prolific flowerbeds, Tivoli fulfils its role as a traditional landscaped garden. It makes an ideal place to sit for lunch or a coffee, away from the bustle of the city. Then, as darkness falls, the atmosphere changes as thousands of electric lights illuminate the park and its Chinese or Moorish-inspired buildings, creating an exotic atmosphere.

Nightlife and Fireworks

Tivoli's 38 bars and restaurants are favourite meeting places for friends, families and business people. It can be difficult getting a seat at some of the restaurants on warm summer evenings, and it's advisable to book in advance or make a reservation when you arrive at the park. Some of the venues are situated around the perimeter and are accessible when the park is closed.

There's no shortage of evening entertainment. The open-air stage is the focus for spectacular productions such as *A Tivoli Fairytale* celebrating Hans Christian Andersen. On

...day evenings it is the venue for pop and rock concerts ...eaturing bands from Denmark and abroad. And on Wednesday and Saturday at 11.45pm it becomes the setting for the eagerly awaited fireworks display – a Tivoli institution.

Other shows include a son-et-lumière at Tivoli lake (daily, 15 mins before closing). The lake is all that remains of a moat which surrounded the old town until 1856.

Jazz, blues and swing are all on the programme at Tivoli over the summer. For classical music, check out the main Concert Hall, home of the Sjællands Symphony Orchestra. Many of the performances are free. The hall was built in 1956 and has recently undergone major renovation work.

Rollercoaster Rides

No pleasure park is complete without its amusements. Among the most popular are the old-style wooden rollercoaster, ferris wheel and the merry-go-rounds. A multi-ride ticket can be purchased at the entrance or from machines around the park.

The Man Who Made Tivoli

The driving force behind Tivoli was the 19th-century polyglot entrepreneur Georg Cartensen. He had travelled widely and seen the idea in practice in cities such as Paris. His vision was to combine a pleasure garden with venues for cultural events and a fair. But first he had to persuade the king, Christian VIII, of his plan's viability. The king gave his assent 'to provide the masses with suitable entertainment and fun', and Tivoli opened its doors to the public in August 1843. Crowds flocked to the gardens to see pantomimes, shows and fireworks displays and enjoy the rides, fairground stalls and concerts. Among the first attractions was a cable-car ride. Over the years, Tivoli has been modernised and extended, but its magic is undiminished and it still retains a special place in the hearts of the Danes.

Thrilling rides are all part of the fun at Tivoli

Tivoli Boys' Guard

Following a tradition that goes back to the 19th century, the Tivoli Boys' Guard parades through the park on Saturday and Sunday, dressed in red and white uniforms and bearskin caps, playing military music. The enthusiasm of this royal guard in miniature more than compensates for any lack of musical experience.

Louis Tussaud's Wax Museum

Housed in a Renaissance villa bordering Tivoli on Hans Christian Andersens Boulevard is **Louis Tussaud's Wax Museum** (open daily 10am–6pm; admission fee; <www.tussaud.dk>). Wax models of more than 200 Danish and foreign personalities from the worlds of politics, show business and history, including the Nordic royal families, are on display. And for those who can pluck up the courage, there is a Chamber of Horrors, too.

STRØGET AND BEYOND

One of the first places you'll visit after Rådhuspladsen is Copenhagen's most famous pedestrian-only street. Known as Strøget (pronounced stroy-et), this is a continuation of four streets: Frederiksberggade – leading off Rådhuspladsen – Nygade Vimmelskaftet, Amagertorv and Østergade, that wind their way for 1km (about ⅔ mile) to Kongens Nytorv square. This traffic-free haven offers visitors an amazingly eclectic array of shops along with numerous small bars, restaurants, cafés and an abundance of street performers. Don't be afraid to wander off Strøget to explore the small side streets. Each of these has its own surprises among the numerous antiques shops, speciality stores, boutiques and fashionable restaurants.

Strøget

That said, it must also be stated that the entrance to Frederiksberggade, dominated as it is by fast-food outlets, is not exactly prepossessing; however, perseverance will bring its rewards. Where Frederiksberggade ends, Strøget opens out into two squares on either side of the street. **Gammeltorv**, to the left, is a popular place for small market stalls and is home to the **Caritas Fountain** which, dating from 1610, is the city's oldest. In a tradition going back to the golden wedding of King Christian IX and Queen Louise in 1892, imitation golden apples are made to dance on the jets of the fountain on the monarch's birthday (now 16 April). **Nytorv,**

Strøget musician

Royal Copenhagen Porcelain

to the right, is dominated by the impressive architecture of the law courts. Each of these squares is a good place to sit at a street café and watch the procession of passing people.

The next place of note is the **Helligåndskirken** (Church of the Holy Spirit). Built in the 17th–18th century, it is set in its own small gardens. Outside is an area particularly popular with street performers and other hawkers. Just past this point, Strøget opens out again and on the left side of Amagertorv you'll see a fine example of Dutch baroque buildings – home to the group of **Royal Copenhagen** shops *(see page 85)*. One of these, at No. 6, is the Royal Copenhagen Porcelain store, an Aladdin's cave with an elegant restaurant and small museum. It dates from 1616. Next door, Georg Jensen features tableware sets designed over the last century. For the best of Danish design, pop in to Illums Bolighus at No. 10, an elegant department store featuring kitchenware, lighting and furniture.

A few steps further, at the junction of Amagertorv and Østergade, another busy pedestrian-only shopping street, Købmagergade, leads off to the left. At No. 24 is the **Museum Erotica** (open May–Sept daily 10am–11pm; Oct–Apr Sun–Thur 11am–8pm, Fri–Sat 10am–10pm; admission fee; <www.museumerotica.dk>). It claims to be the world's first serious erotic museum and was opened 25 years after pornography was legalised in Denmark in 1968.

> **Museum Erotica is not simply a display of nude bodies, but a celebration of how eroticism and sexuality have been expressed since ancient times. The exhibits become more explicit floor by floor.**

Back on Strøget, now called Østergade, the shops are more upmarket and include the likes of Gianni Versace and Bang & Olufsen. Pause to look in the window of Halberstadt (No. 4) – a jeweller founded in 1846 – which features a small train encrusted with gems that runs continually around.

Around Kongens Nytorv

Kongens Nytorv, the 'King's New Square' of Christian V – dating from 1680 and still the city's largest (12 streets lead off it) – is surrounded by impressive stately buildings. The park in the centre of the square is dominated by the king himself, in the form of an elaborate equestrian statue of Christian V, with four classical figures seated submissively under his horse.

On the southwest side is **Det Kongelige Teater** (Danish Royal Theatre; <www.kglteater.dk>), one of the country's most important cultural centres. Home of Danish national ballet, opera and drama, it was originally opened in 1748, rebuilt in 1874, and was briefly the stage of Hans Christian Andersen at the age of 14, who tried without success to become a ballet dancer. The theatre is now complemented by the new state-of-the-art Copenhagen Opera House, which also houses the company's ballet performances *(see page 66)*.

Next to the theatre stands **Charlottenborg Slot**, the oldest building on the square. It was built as a royal palace in 1683 in the style of Dutch baroque and, since 1754, has been the home of the Royal Academy of Fine Arts. Enter through the front gate and at the rear is **Charlottenborg Udstillings-bygning**, which exhibits Danish and international contemporary art (open daily 10am–5pm, Wed till 7pm; admission fee; <www.charlottenborg-art.dk>).

Look around the square and you will notice other splendid buildings. **Thotts Palae** (Thott's Mansion) in the northeast corner, was built for the naval hero Admiral Niels Juel and is now home to the French Embassy. Not to be outdone is the wonderful façade of the five-star **Hotel D'Angleterre**, one of Denmark's finest hotels.

Kongens Nytorv with the statue of Christian V

The unusually shaped building tucked between Store Strandstræde and Bredgage is the beautifully preserved 1782 **Kanneworffs Hus**, which houses Ravhuset, a shop selling jewellery made from Baltic amber; located above Ravhuset is a small **Amber Museum** (open May–Aug daily 10am–8pm, Sept–Apr daily 10am–6pm; admission fee; <www.houseofamber.com>). Diagonally across the square is the imposing **Magasin du Nord** with its impressive ornate façade. This was Scandinavia's first department store and is still its largest.

South of Strøget

Leave Kongens Nytorv by Vingårdsstraede at the southwest corner of Magasin du Nord. You'll find yourself in an area of jazz clubs, small bars and artists' hangouts. At its junction with Admiralgade is the massive 70-m (230-ft) tall copper spire of **Skt Nicolai Kirke** (St Nicholas Church). Destroyed several times by fire and rebuilt as recently as 1917, it houses the Copenhagen Contemporary Art Centre, **Kunsthallen Nikolaj** (open daily noon–5pm; admission fee, Wed free; <www.kunsthallennikolaj.dk>), which has a small permanent collection and an innovative programme of temporary exhibitions. At the south end of Admiralgade is **Holmens Kirke** (open Mon–Sat 9am–noon, until 2pm in summer; admission free). The church is in the Venetian style, but with Dutch gable ends and a small copper tower in the middle. The building was originally a 16th-century anchor forge, but was transformed in 1619 by Christian IV into a sailors' church. On the altar, reredos and pulpit there is a profusion of oak

> **Holmens Kirke remains a favourite with the royal family. In 1967 Queen Margrethe was married here to Prince Henrik, formerly the French Count de Laborde de Montpezat.**

Holmens Kirke, the sailors' church

carvings by Abel Schrøder the Younger. An adjoining chapel (built 1706–8) is dedicated to maritime heroes. Look for the model ship hanging from the ceiling, a tradition common in many Danish churches.

Outside Holmens Kirke you are now by the canal, and it is impossible not to be impressed by the Christiansborg complex on the opposite bank *(see page 38)*. Turn right up Ved Stranden and head for the Højbro bridge and the junction with Gammelstrand and Højbro Plads.

Within a short distance of here are three very different statues. The most obvious of these, on **Højbro Plads**, is the magnificent copper green **equestrian statue of Bishop Absalon** showing the warrior-priest in chain mail with axe in hand. On the corner of Gammelstrand stands the **statue of the Fiskerkone** (Fisherman's Wife), scarf on her head, shawl around her shoulders, wearing an apron and clasping a fish. Erected in 1940, she resembles the women who sit in-

ir stalls nearby every Tuesday–Friday morning, as
men's wives have done here for centuries. The third
ulpture is less obvious; in fact, you'll have to look over the
bridge to discover the submerged depiction of the 'Mermaid
with Seven Sons' that is attractively illuminated at night.

Gammelstrand

Next, turn into Gammelstrand itself; the name means 'old
shore' and, as this implies, it is the former edge of the city.
This is one of the two principal starting points for canal-boat
tours, the other being in Nyhavn *(see page 46)*. Immediately
across the canal lies a distinctive square-arched, yellow-

Vandkunsten square

ochre building with a classi-
cal-style frieze, looking like
a national tomb: a monu-
ment to the great Danish
sculptor Bertel Thorvaldsen
(1770–1844; *see page 41*).
Off to the right, on Frederiksholms Kanal, you'll be able
to make out the arched
entrance to the colossal
Nationalmuseet *(see page
44)*. Gammelstrand also has
restaurants and bars, among
which is the elegant **Krogs**,
one of the city's finest
seafood restaurants.

Time now to proceed
back to Rådhuspladsen, via
a collection of interesting
old streets. At the western
end of Gammelstrand,
Snaregade features some

timber-framed houses. Continuing into Magstræde and the houses at numbers 17 and 19 are two of the city's oldest, dating from 1640. Next is **Vandkunsten**, a delightful little square with outdoor cafés and a pretty fountain. The name of the square means 'water artifice' and it is here that

> Give your feet a rest with a trip on the harbour bus, which connects the Royal Library's Black Diamond building with the Little Mermaid, stopping at Holmen, Nyhavn and the Opera House en route.

Copenhagen's first water pipes were laid. Continue across the next junction into Gåsegade, and look for the gabled houses with 18th-century hoists at the top. Furniture is traditionally hauled up by these hoists, rather than being squeezed up the narrow stairwells.

On the corner of Hestemøllestræde and Lavendelstræde is a house where Mozart's widow lived with her second husband, a Danish diplomat. Here, the huge archways of Copenhagen's fourth town hall dominate; built between 1805 and 1815, it now houses the law courts. On Lavendelstræde you'll find typical Danish houses and shops from 1796, the year after the city's second great fire, and at the end of the street Vester Voldgade leads to Rådhuspladsen.

ON AND AROUND SLOTSHOLMEN

Starting at Rådhuspladsen, retrace your steps on the previous tour back to the Højbro bridge and then cross it to the small island of Slotsholmen (Castle Island) and the imposing towers of Christiansborg. Stop a little further along the canal at the highly ornamented **Børsen** (Stock Exchange), dating from the days of Christian IV. Its green copper roof is topped by a spire composed of four entwined dragon's tails. Christian IV was influenced by the booming Netherlands architec-

...ure of his day, and in 1619 commissioned two Dutch brothers to design the building. Currently it houses special events, and the Stock Exchange has since emigrated to Strøget.

Christiansborg and its Museums

Christiansborg is the sixth castle or palace to have stood on this site since Absalon built his fortress in 1167: pillage, fire and rebuilding frenzies have taken their toll on the earlier ones. The third castle became the permanent seat of the king and government in 1417. The present edifice dates from the early 20th century, at which time Thorvald Jørgensen won an architectural competition for the design of a new Christiansborg palace. On 15 November 1907, King Frederik VIII laid the cornerstone that had been hewn out of the granite remains from Absalon's original castle. Above this a vast plinth was made of 7,500 boulders donated by 750 Danish boroughs, and

Christiansborg, seat of the Danish Parliament

then the palace was faced with granite slabs. Look up to see 57 granite masks of Denmark's greatest men. Covered in copper between 1937 and 1939, the roof of Christiansborg makes an imposing addition to the city's verdigris skyline.

The chapel, theatre museum, riding stables and beautifully restored **Marmorbroen** (Marble Bridge) that sur-

Marble Bridge, built in 1745

vived two disastrous fires in 1794 and 1884 help to give the palace a more venerable aspect than its more recent origins suggest. Today the castle houses government ministries, Parliament (Folketing) and the Danish Supreme Court, as well as being the centre of a complex of museums.

The most notable highlights of the complex include the **Kongelige Repræsentationslokaler** (Royal Reception Chambers; guided tours in English: May–Sept daily 11am, 1pm and 3pm, Oct–Apr Tues–Sun 3pm; admission fee; tel: 33 92 64 92; <www.ses.dk>). One of the guide's first anecdotes will most probably be: 'Look at the roof here, held by pillars in the shape of male statues, heads bent to take the weight – a symbol of modern Danes paying their taxes…'

The chambers, situated on the first floor, are used by the Queen and Prime Minister for official receptions, state banquets, and royal audiences with foreign ambassadors. They are richly decorated with works of art retrieved from the earlier palaces, as well as pieces by modern Danish artists. Most impressive is the 40-m (130-ft) long Great Hall hung with a series of tapestries by Bjørn Nørgaard recounting the history of Denmark. The tapestries were commissioned by the Danish business community to mark the occasion of Queen Margrethe II's 50th birthday in 1990 and were made by Les Gobelins in Paris. They took 10 years to complete. Other chambers include the Throne Room and the balcony overlooking Slotspladsen (Castle Square), from where monarchs are proclaimed.

In the palace basement you will find the extensive **Ruinerne af Absalons Borg** (Ruins of Absalon's Palace; open May–Sept daily 10am–4pm, closed 2 and 14 May; Oct–Apr Tues–Sun 10am–4pm; admission fee; tel: 33 92 64 92 for tours), from 1167, as well as remnants of more recent castles on the site. Also in the complex is the **Folketing** (Danish Parliament; for tours tel: 33 37 55 00; <www.folketinget.dk>).

Out in the vast parade ground, dominated by a copper equestrian statue of Christian IX, are the **Kongelige Stalde og Kareter** (Royal Stables; open Jan–Apr Sat–Sun 2–4pm;

A royal carriage on display in Christiansborg's stables

May–Sept Fri–Sun 2–4pm; admission fee). The stables are home to some fine driving and riding horses, which can sometimes be seen exercising in the square. On display are uniforms and royal state carriages dating from 1778.

Theatre Museum

Situated in an elegant terrace above the stables is the **Teatermuseet** (Theatre Museum; open Tues–Thur 11am–3pm, Wed till 5pm, Sat–Sun 1–4pm; admisson

Sculptor Bertel Thorvaldsen's distinctive museum

fee; <www.teatermuseet.dk>). The delightful little auditorium and galleries are packed with Danish and international theatrical relics – memorabilia of Ibsen, Anna Pavlova and Hans Christian Andersen, as well as playbills, costumes and photographs of the country's theatrical history.

Thorvaldsens Museum

A museum of classical intent occupies the Gammelstrand side of the Christiansborg complex, but the Roman and Greek gods gazing down at you are all 19th-century revivals of antiquity. **Thorvaldsens Museum** (open Tues–Sun 10am–5pm; guided tours in English July–Aug Sun 3pm; admission fee, Wed free; <www.thorvaldsensmuseum.dk>) is dedicated to the celebrated Danish sculptor Bertel Thorvaldsen (1770–1844). At the tender age of 11 the young Bertel was accepted by the Copenhagen Art Academy. Later he won a scholarship to Rome, where he lived and worked

Cannon in the Arsenal Museum

for more than 40 years. Returning to Denmark in triumph, Thorvaldsen devoted his library, collection and fortune to the creation of a museum of his own works. He chose a young architect, Gottlieb Bindesbøll, to design it. The result is one of Copenhagen's most distinctive buildings, with a decorated ochre façade, and interior walls and ceilings in black, reds, blues and oranges, contrasting with the pure white plaster and marble of Thorvaldsen's sculptures.

Arsenal Museum

In a side street behind the Royal Stables, **Tøjhusmuseet** (Arsenal Museum; open Tues–Sun noon–4pm, closed 23–26, 31 Dec and 1 Jan; admission fee; <www.thm.dk>) holds a fascinating collection of military items, including an early 15th-century cannon from the time of Queen Margrete I and sophisticated modern weapons. Attendants wearing three-cornered hats and knee-length red jackets greet you as you enter the vast 400-year-old building. Cannonballs are piled high like potatoes and old military planes are suspended from the roof. Upstairs there is a glittering array of uniforms and small arms.

Royal Library

Close by are the **Library Gardens**. Designed in 1920, the gardens are a veritable oasis of peace and calm, and an ideal place to sit and rest. Although the building you see from the gardens only dates from 1906, Frederik III founded the **Det**

Kongelige Bibliotek (Royal Library, <www.kb.dk>) around 1653. Later it was merged with the University Library, founded in 1482. Walk around the building to the waterfront and be prepared for a huge architectural surprise. On Søren Kierkegaards Plads a seven-storey, glass, granite, concrete and steel structure appears to be leaning towards the river. This, because of its colour, is affectionately known as **Den Sorte Diamant** (The Black Diamond), and is the annexe for the Royal Library. Concerts, lectures and meetings are also held here, and there are excellent shops, restaurants and cafés.

An architectural masterpiece on a very different scale is Daniel Libeskind's conversion of the Royal Boat House into the **Dansk Jødisk Museum** (Danish Jewish Museum, Proviantpassagen 6; open winter Tues–Fri 1–4pm, Sat Sun noon–5pm; summer Tues–Sun 10am–5pm; admission fee; <www.jewmus.dk>). This unexpected find in the Royal

The tranquil gardens of the Royal Library

> The word *mitzvah* on the door of the Danish Jewish Museum means 'a good deed'. It relates to the remarkable rescue in 1943 of 7,000 Jews who, in the face of deportation to Nazi concentration camps, were hidden and taken in small boats to Sweden.

Library Gardens tells the story of Denmark's Jews, their cultural heritage and daily life, through its collection of paintings, photographs, artefacts, memoirs, films and audio recordings.

National Museum

Leaving Slotsholmen by the Marble Bridge, turn right and follow the canal to Ny Vestergade and the **Nationalmuseet** (National Museum; Tues–Sun 10am–5pm; free; <www.natmus.dk>). The biggest museum in Scandinavia, it focuses on Danish history from the Stone Age to modern times. One of the most striking exhibits is the Trundholm Sun Chariot (1200BC), dating from a period when the Danes worshipped the sun, imagining it as a disc of gold riding through the sky in a chariot behind a celestial horse. Other sections of the museum contain ethnographic exhibits from around the world – including a reconstructed Inuit camp from Greenland – classical antiquities and the Royal Coin and Medal Collection. A hands-on Children's Museum provides an interesting diversion for youngsters.

Ny Carlsberg Glyptotek

From the Nationalmuseet, cross over Hans Christian Andersens Boulevard and head for the distinctive classical building with a columned portal and domed roof, which houses **Ny Carlsberg Glyptotek** (Dantes Plads 7; open Tues–Sun 10am–4pm; admission fee, Sun free; <www.glyptoteket.dk>). The Glyptotek was founded on the classical collection of Carl Jacobsen (1842–1914), a Danish brewer and art connoisseur. Under its elaborate roof lies one of the world's foremost displays of Egyptian, Greek, Roman and Etruscan art. A sub-tropical garden in the central hall appears to have been transplanted directly from ancient Rome. In contrast, the French collection – works by Gauguin, van Gogh and Monet, Rodin sculptures and a complete set of Degas bronzes – is housed in a glorious spacious new wing.

Danish Design Centre

To see the latest in modern design classics, for which Denmark is justly renowned, cross the road to the **Dansk Design Center** (Hans Christian Andersens Boulevard 27; open Mon–Fri 10am–5pm, Wed till 9pm, Sat–Sun 11am–4pm; admission fee; <www.ddc.dk>). You will see the country's preoccupation with cool, clean, elegant lines.

The domed roof and sub-tropical garden of Ny Carlsberg Glyptotek

NYHAVN AND BEYOND

➤ This walk begins at Kongens Nytorv (bus 26 from Rådhus-pladsen). Cross the square towards **Nyhavn**; the name liter-ally means 'new harbour' and immediately you'll notice the nautical flavour of this one-time 'sailors' street'. Over the centuries the two sides of the canal have developed into a re-markable illustration of old Copenhagen. At the Kongens Nytorv end of the canal, which was dug in 1671 to enlarge the harbour, stands a sizeable old anchor, a memorial to the Danish sailors killed in World War II. On either side of the canal itself, an unusual collection of vessels lies at anchor

Colourful Nyhavn

with their masts colourfully be-decked with the Danish flag. This sight, combined with numerous restaurants and bars with outside terraces, and the antiques shops and other stores on the north side, draws thousands of people who are only too happy to eat, drink and socialise in such an at-tractive and lively setting.

This is a street with everything – history, architecture, nightlife, a constant passage of colourful small vessels. It was even home to Hans Christian Andersen, who lived here first at number 67 from 1854–64 and later at number 18.

Walk along Nyhavn on the north side, and you'll pass a superb hotel conversion of an 18th-century warehouse. Just beyond is a view over the inner harbour to the Christianshavn area where the spiralling steeple of Vor Frelsers Kirke dominates the skyline *(see page 64)*.

Amaliehavn Gardens

Turn left and walk along the waterfront and then bear left to Skt Annæ Plads. This is a fine boulevard lined with con-sulates and distinguished old offices, but rather than follow it, turn right and walk along the waterfront to the pleasant **Amaliehavn Gardens**. These were created by Belgian land-scape architect Jean Delogne in 1983 using French lime-stone and Danish granite. The bronze pillars around the

fountain were designed by Italian sculptor Arnaldo Pomo-
doro. Across the water you'll see the magnificent new Opera
House, opened in 2005 *(see page 66)*.

Amalienborg Palace

The road leading away from the water takes you to one of the
most attractively symmetrical squares in Europe, **Amalienborg Plads**. The huge equestrian statue of Frederik V, unveiled
in 1771 and dominating the centre of the square, gives you a
clue that you are now in the proximity of royalty. In fact, the
four identical mansions (at least on their exterior) that line the
octagonal perimeter of the square were originally constructed
in 1749 as town mansions for four noblemen. After Christiansborg Palace was destroyed by fire for the second time in 1794,
the royal family slowly began buying Amalienborg from the
nobles, and has lived here since. Today, collectively known as

Amalienborg Plads and Palace, home of the royal family

Amalienborg Slot (Palace), these buildings are considered to be one of the finest rococo ensembles in Europe.

Four roads converge at right angles on the courtyard, while bearskin-clad soldiers guard each of the palaces and corners, with an extra sentry posted at the gateway between the two palaces to your left. The wing to the left of the colonnade is Christian IX's Palace, the winter residence of Queen Margrethe. On the

On duty at Amalienborg

right of the colonnade, **Christian VII's Palace** (guided tours in English July–Sept Sat–Sun 1pm; admission fee; <www.ses.dk>) is used for receptions and to house royal guests.

Continuing around the square, the third building, Christian VIII's Palace is the home of Crown Prince Frederik. The palace also houses the **Amalienborg Palace Museum** (open Nov–Apr Tues–Sun 11am–4pm; May–Oct daily 10am–4pm; closed 18–26, 31 Dec and 1 Jan; admission fee; <www.ses.dk>) where the Royal Collection is on show in the splendid private apartments of the Danish Glücksborg kings from 1863 to 1947. Among the exhibits are the treasured works of art given to Christian IX (reigned 1863–1906) and Queen Louise by their six children, some of whom married into other leading European royal families. The fourth building is Frederik VIII's Palace. The name Amalienborg came from the wife of Frederik III, Queen Sophie Amalie.

The main attraction at Amalienborg when the Queen is in residence is the daily **Changing of the Guard**. At 11.30am

Wartime memorabilia at Frihedsmuseet

the guards leave their barracks near Rosenborg Castle *(see page 60)* in formation, and march through the city streets so as to arrive in the palace square just before noon, moving from one sentry-box to another in a series of foot-stamping ceremonies. Guardsmen march to the accompaniment of a band, their black bearskins rippling in the breeze. They wear blue trousers with white stripes and highly polished boots; on festive occasions they dress in red tunics with white shoulder straps.

Churchill Park

Leave the square via Amaliegade and follow it north for about 730m (800yd) to its junction with Esplanaden. Churchill Parken is on the opposite side of the road and has several interesting sights.

The **Frihedsmuseet** (Museum of the Danish Resistance Movement 1940–45; open May–Sept Tues–Sat 10am–4pm, Sun and holidays 10am–5pm; Oct–Apr Tues–Sat 10am–3pm, Sun and holidays 10am–4pm; free; <www.natmus.dk>) is located at one of the prettiest spots in the city – especially in springtime when the daffodils are in bloom. The museum provides a graphic record of wartime tragedy during the German occupation. Displays illustrate the daring exploits of the Resistance Movement.

Just beyond, the Anglican **St Alban's Church** (<www.st-albans.dk>) looks as if it has been transplanted from an English country village. It was indeed constructed amid the green lawns of Churchill Park in 1887 by an English architect. On a small slope next to the church there is a sight that is guaranteed to hold your attention. Copenhagen has numerous fountains but this, the **Gefion Fountain**, is the most spectacular. It was commissioned by the Carlsberg Foundation, and in 1908 sculptor Anders Bundgaard's depiction of the legend of the Nordic goddess Gefion – who turned her four sons into oxen and used them to pull the island of Zealand from Sweden – was unveiled.

The Little Mermaid

Follow the right-hand path through delightful gardens past the fountain to Langelinie, and there on the water's edge you will see the most famous statue of all, **Den Lille**
Havfrue (the Little Mermaid). In Andersen's fairytale, this tragic sea-girl exchanged her voice for human legs in order

Edvard Eriksen's Little Mermaid, modelled on his wife

to gain the love of an earthly prince, but mutely had to watch as he jilted her for a real princess. In desperation, she threw herself into the sea and turned into foam. To the dismay of both visitors and Danes, the mermaid has frequently been vandalised. Fortunately, the workshop of sculptor Edvard Eriksen retains the original moulds from 1913, and new parts can be cast if necessary. Although famous, it must be said that the statue is rather small compared to the photographs that often depict it at the mouth of the harbour.

The Citadel

After viewing the Little Mermaid, take the road running inland from the water, cross a bridge and descend the flight of steps on the left. This leads to a wooden bridge on the far side of which is the **Kastellet** (Citadel), a star-shaped fortress with five bastions. It was begun by Frederik III in 1662. Building continued until 1725 and today the fortress is still in use by the army – the church, prison and main guardhouse having resisted the assaults of time. It is a delightfully peaceful enclave, with a charming windmill (1847) and some remains of the old ramparts well worth seeing.

All quiet at the Citadel

Leave by the wooden bridge leading south into Churchill Parken, and then turn right onto Esplanaden. Cross Store Kongensgade into Gernersgade and you are in the heart of Nyboder (New Dwellings) whose long rows of houses were built between 1631 and 1641 by Christian IV as dwellings for his sailors. Painted yellow-ochre, with steep gabled roofs and

Twentieth-century design icons, the Museum of Decorative Art

shuttered windows, they form a fashionable, well-preserved community of homes still inhabited by navy personnel. **Nyboders Mindestuer** (St Pauls Gade 24; open Wed 11am–2pm, Sun 11am–4pm; admission fee; <www.orlogsmuseet.dk/nybod22.htm>), a small museum, shows the cramped rooms of a typical 19th-century family and a small naval exhibition.

A Stroll Along Bredgade

Backtrack to Bredgade and turn right. The area from here to Kongens Nytorv is a residential quarter of substantial granite houses and quadrangles. It was planned by architect Nicolai Eigtved at about the same time as Amalienborg. At number 68 you'll find the **Kunstindustrimuseet** (Museum of Decorative Art; Bredgade 68 (open Tues–Fri 10am–4pm, Wed till 6pm; Sat–Sun noon–4pm; admission fee; <www.kunstindustrimuseet.dk>). Housed in an attractive rococo building (a former hospital) dating from 1757, the museum focuses

Frederik V's grandiose Marble Church, modelled on St Peter's, Rome

on Danish and European decorative art, along with Oriental handicrafts dating from the Middle Ages to the present. Summer performances of Shakespeare (in Danish) are held in the splendid garden.

On one side of the museum, at number 70, there is a plaque commemorating the death of the philosopher Søren Kierkegaard *(see opposite)* in 1855. On the other side, at number 64, is Skt Ansgars Kirke, centre of the modest Roman Catholic community since 1842. A museum documents the history of Catholicism in the city since its virtual extinction in the Reformation of 1536. Immediately after the church stands the fascinating **Medicinsk Historisk Museum** (Medical Museum; guided tours only, in English July–Aug Sun 2pm; admission fee; <www.museion.ku.dk>). Then it comes as a surprise to see, across the road, the golden onion-shaped domes of Alexander Nevsky Kirke, built for the Russian Orthodox community in 1883.

Marble Church

A few steps further and the great dome of the **Marmor-kirken** (Marble Church; open Mon–Thur 10am–5pm, Wed till 6pm, Fri–Sun and holidays noon–5pm; free; visits to the dome Sept–June Sat–Sun 1 and 3pm, June–Aug daily 1 and 3pm; admission fee; <www.marmorkirken.dk>), officially called the Frederiks Kirken, rises high to your right. Measuring 31m (100ft) in diameter, this is one of the largest church domes in Europe. The cornerstone was laid by Frederik V in 1749. However, the Norwegian marble required for the building became so expensive that the project was halted. It was eventually completed using Danish marble and consecrated in 1894.

Inside, the dome is decorated with rich frescoes in blue, gold and green, representing the Apostles. Outside, the building is surrounded by statues of personalities of the Danish Church, including St Ansgar, who helped to bring Christianity to Denmark, and Grundtvig, the 19th-century educationalist. On the roof are 16 religious figures, from Moses to Luther. Continue along Bredgade to Kongens Nytorv past an array of boutiques, antiques shops and galleries.

Søren Kierkegaard

The top-hatted figure of Søren Kierkegaard (1813–55) was a familiar sight to Copenhagers as he took his daily walk along the city's cobbled streets. Regarded as one of the founders of Existentialism, Kierkegaard's philosophy developed out of personal anguish and his distaste for organised religion. You'll find a small exhibition devoted to Kierkegaard at Københavns Bymuseum (Copenhagen City Museum, Vesterbrogade 59; open Thur–Mon 10am–4pm, Wed 10am–9pm; tel: 33 21 07 72; admission fee; <www.bymuseum.dk>), a ten-minute walk west from Radhuspladsen along Vesterbrogade.

Picturesque Gråbørdretorv

UNIVERSITY QUARTER AND PARKS

From Rådhuspladsen, go northwest for a short way along Vester Voldgade and then turn right into narrow Studiestræde, home to a melange of antiques shops, bookstalls and boutiques gathered in an 18th-century setting.

At Studiestræde 6 a plaque records that H.C. Ørsted, who discovered electro-magnetism in 1820, lived here. A few metres further on, at the corner of Nørregade, you will see one of Copenhagen's oldest preserved buildings, the former Bispegården (Bishop's Residence), built in 1500 and now part of the university. Nearby on Bispetorvet, a monument erected in 1943 commemorates the 400th anniversary of the introduction of the Reformation to Denmark.

Copenhagen Cathedral

At the end of Studiestræde stands the **Domkirke** (Cathedral) of Copenhagen, known as **Vor Frue Kirke** (Church of Our Lady). Bishop Absalon's successor, Sunesen, is said to have laid its foundations in the 12th century, but by 1316 it had already burned down four times. Later, two further constructions were destroyed – by the great 1728 fire and by British bombardment in 1807. The present church was reconstructed by V.F.K. and C.F. Hansen between 1811 and 1829. Its austere interior is relieved by a collection of heroic statues by Bertel Thorvaldsen: 12 massive marble Apostles line the aisle, while an orange-lit altar is surrounded by bronze candelabra and dominated by his figure of Christ.

University and Gråbørdretorv

Proceed along the north side of the Cathedral. On the left is the main Copenhagen University block, which dates back in its present form only as far as the 1830s. The university was founded in 1479. This is a typical student area with a number of interesting bookshops and cafés.

Turn right into Fiolstræde, a lively spot for alfresco dining, and left into Skindergade, which leads into **Gråbørdretorv** (Greyfriar's Square), a large, picturesque traffic-free square surrounded by brightly painted 18th-century houses. It was the site of a Franciscan monastery until the Reformation. Cafés and restaurants have proliferated here in recent years.

Round Tower

Continue along Skindergade to Købmagergade and you'll find yourself at the foot of one of Copenhagen's most beloved landmarks, the ▶ **Rundetaarn** (Round Tower;

> The Rundetaarn (Round Tower) has the oldest functioning observatory in Europe. It's open on Sunday, late June–mid-Aug, 1–4pm. In winter, you can view the night sky through its telescope (Oct–Mar, Tues and Wed 7–10pm).

open June–Aug Mon–Sat 10am–8pm, Sun noon–8pm; Sept–May Mon–Sat 10am–5pm, Sun noon–5pm; admission fee; <www.rundetaarn.dk>). The Round Tower was built by Christian IV in 1642 as part of his vision to provide an astronomical observatory, church and university library for 17th-century scholars. You can walk to the top of the 36-m (118-ft) high tower, but not by any ordinary means – steps would have been impractical for raising the heavy equipment needed here. Instead, a wide spiral ramp, 210m (690ft) long, winds around inside the tower. Not only did Tsar Peter the Great ride up to the top on horseback in 1716, but his empress followed him in a horse-drawn coach. There is a splendid view over the rooftops of the old city from the top. **Trinitatis Kirke** (Trinity Church) is to the rear of the tower; the library hall above is now used for exhibitions and concerts.

A spiral ramp winds 7½ times around the inside of the Round Tower

The building across Køb-magergade from the Round Tower, at the corner with Krystalgade, is the Regensen university hostel. Although students have lived here since 1623 most of the present structure dates from the 18th century. The notable addition is an arcade built in 1909. A couple of hundred metres along Krystalgade stands the Synagogue of Copenhagen. It was inaugurated in 1833.

Musikhistorisk Museum

Musical Interlude

From the Round Tower, turn left onto pleasant Købmagergade, which is one of Copenhagen's oldest commercial thoroughfares. At number 37 you'll find the **Post & Tele Museum** (Post and Telecommunications Museum; open Tues, Thur–Sat 10am–5pm, Wed 10am–8pm, Sun noon–4pm; admission fee; <www.ptt-museum.dk>). Look out for the ice boat which was used to transport mail across the Great Belt. The museum has an excellent roof-top café.

Backtrack to the Round Tower and turn right into Landemærket. Two blocks along on the left, on Åbenrå, music lovers will find an attraction certainly worth a visit: **Musikmuseet** (Danish Music Museum, Åbenrå 30; open May–Sept Tues–Sun 1–3.50pm, Oct–Apr Tues, Wed, Sat, Sun 1–3.50pm; free; <www.natmus.dk>) focuses on the history of musical instruments in Europe from 1000 to 1900. It has a collection of 3,800 instruments from around the world, with a special hands-on percussion room for kids.

Rosenborg Slot

On the opposite side of Kronprinsessegade, **Kongens Have** (King's Garden) was laid out in 1606–34 by Christian IV who found Christiansborg Palace too official and oppressive. In warm weather, the area attracts many sunbathers, picnickers and families. He built himself a small country mansion in a corner of the site, outside the town walls. This he eventually expanded into the three-storey Dutch Renaissance-style **Rosenborg Slot** (Rosenborg Castle; open Nov–Apr Tues–Sun 11am–4pm; May, Sept and Oct daily 10am–4pm; June–Aug daily 10am–5pm; admission fee; <www.rosenborgslot.dk>; *see picture on page 15*). Rosenborg became home for the next three generations of kings until Frederik IV erected Frederiksberg Castle in 1710. Since 1838 it has been a royal museum of considerable grace and home of the crown jewels.

Formal gardens around Rosenborg Slot

The castle's 24 rooms are arranged chronologically, beginning with Christian IV's tower-room study, which is still furnished in its original style. The Long Hall, with tapestries of the Swedish Wars, ornate ceiling and three almost life-siz silver lions, contains one of the world's largest collections of silver furniture, mostly from the 18th century.

> **The Order of the Elephant is Denmark's highest decoration. Instituted by Christian V in 1693, the insignia is worn by members of the royal family and can be bestowed upon foreign heads of state. Britain's Queen Elizabeth II is a member of the Order.**

The crown jewels are held in the treasury. In addition to the oldest existing insignia of the Order of the Elephant *(see panel above)*, there are 18 cases of crowns, gilded swords, precious stones and coronation cups – even royal inkwells and tea sets in pure gold. The centrepiece of this regal room is the 17th-century crown of the absolute monarchy – made out of gold, with diamonds, two sapphires and ruby spinels.

Visiting gardeners will be particularly interested in the **Botanisk Have** (Botanical Gardens; open daily May–Sept 8.30am–6pm; Oct–Apr Tues–Sun 8.30am–4pm; free; <www.botanic-garden.ku.dk>), located behind Rosenborg Slot, across Øster Voldgade. It has Denmark's largest collection of living plants.

Fine Arts Museum

Art lovers should allow themselves time to explore the **Statens Museum for Kunst** (Fine Arts Museum; Sølvgade 48–50; open Tues–Sun 10am–5pm, Wed 10am–8pm; free, admission fee for special exhibitions; <www.smk.dk>). Paintings from early Dutch to modern Danish, including a large Matisse collection and perhaps the world's finest collection of Dürer prints, are housed in a light and airy building, which reopened at the end of 2006 after an extensive renovation.

Across the park at Stockholmsgade 20 is **Den Hirschsprungske Samling** (Hirschsprung Collection; open Wed–Mon 11am–4pm, closed 23–25, 31 Dec and 1 Jan; admission fee, Wed free; <www.hirschsprung.dk>), a delightful museum packed with to 19th-century Danish painting, sculpture and decorative art. Heinrich Hirschsprung, a tobacco merchant, donated the works to the state in 1902. Look out for the portraits and landscapes of C.W. Eckersberg (1783–1853), whose meticulous style had a far-reaching influence.

It's possible to return to Rådhuspladsen by bus or by train from Nørreport Station. But, if you prefer to walk, there is another surprise: the leafy **Ørsteds Parken**, on the right-hand side of Nørre Voldgade. This charming park offers a wonderful respite during daylight hours.

Carlsberg Brewery

No visit to Copenhagen is complete without sampling the local brew and there is no better place to do this than at Carlsberg Brewery (Gammel Carlsbergvej 11, Valby; open Tues–Sun 10am–4pm; tel: 33 27 12 82; admission fee; <www.visitcarlsberg.com>; buses 18, 26, 6A, and 832). When Jacob Christian Jacobsen (1811–87) inherited his father's small brewery, he set off around Germany in search of the perfect brew and then, with new yeast in hand, he built his brewery on a hill *(berg)* outside the city ramparts. He named his beer Carlsberg after his son, Carl (1842–1914). But father and son did not see eye to eye and Carl opened his own brewery next door. You can find out more about the family – and the beer – at the Visitors' Centre and also tour Carlsberg's latest addition, the Jacobsen Brewhouse micro brewery.

The new Opera House at Holmen

CHRISTIANSHAVN AND HOLMEN

Though there's so much to see within a small radius of Råd-huspladsen and Kongens Nytorv, it's worth spending a few hours across the Knippelsbro bridge in **Christianshavn**. The area was named Christian's Harbour after Christian IV, and it looks like a slice of Amsterdam, reflecting the king's predilection for Dutch architecture.

Christianskirke

Having crossed Knippel Bridge you are on Torvegade. Turn right at the intersection with Strandgade and stroll to the sombre **Christianskirke**. Built in 1755 by Nicolai Eigtved, it possesses an unexpected interior layout with arched galleries reminiscent of an old-time music hall.

Now backtrack and after crossing Torvegade continue on Strandgade until you reach the impressive **Dansk Arkitektur Center** (Danish Architecture Centre; open daily 10am–

5pm; admission fee; <www.dac.dk>), which is located in a former warehouse at Gammel Dok. The area has numerous 17th- and 18th-century houses with cobbled courtyards. N.F.S. Grundtvig *(see page 18)* spent some years at number 4B. Living at number 6 in the early 18th century was Admiral Peter Wessel Tordenskjold – a Danish-Norwegian hero who won battles at sea, but whose exuberant lifestyle ashore lost him many good neighbours. It's said that every time he called *skål* (cheers) during his frequent banquets, a salute would be fired from two cannons at the main doorway, with many a sleepless night had by all until his death in a duel in 1720.

Vor Frelsers Kirke
Follow Skt Annæ Gade from Strandgade towards the distinctive twisted spire of the **Vor Frelsers Kirke** (Church of Our

Copenhagen rooftops from Vor Frelsers Kirke

Saviour), which is closed for a major restoration until at least 2008. The tower may remain open during some or all of this period. See <www.vorfrelserskirke.dk> for further information.

Construction of this brick and sandstone church began in 1682, under the direction of Lambert van Haven; it was consecrated in April 1696. Its most dominant exterior feature, an external spiralling staircase that twists around the tower four times, was designed by Lauridz de

**A spiral staircase surrounds
Vor Frelsers Kirke tower**

Thurah and was dedicated in August 1752. He is said to have been influenced at the time by the Sant'Ivo alla Sapienza Church in Rome. A total of 400 steps, 150 on the outside, lead from the entrance of the church to the gilt globe and Christ figure on top of the spire.

The inside of the church is of interest not simply because of the choir screen, which is guarded by six wooden angels, nor because of the ornate white marble font supported by four cherubs – not even because of the altar dating from 1732, replete with allegorical statues and Dresden-like figures playing in the clouds – but because of the monumental organ, built in 1700 and several times remodelled, on the last occasion in 1965. Beautifully ornamented, the whole construction is supported by two large stucco elephants. The central vault of the church is decorated with a monogram of Christian V, the royal coat of arms and a chain of the Order of the Elephant (see page 61).

Christiania

Outside Vor Frelsers Kirke, turn left onto Prinsessegade and follow the brick wall to a somewhat more esoteric experience. In 1971, a group of local people broke into an abandoned military barracks here and founded **Christiania** free state (guided walks, Sat and Sun 3pm; charge; <www.christiania.org>). Denmark proclaimed it a social experiment soon thereafter, and it has provoked controversy ever since. Around 1,000 people live and work in this community, with its eclectic collection of eateries, wonderful architecture and great concert venue, Loppen. Being an 'alternative' society, there was for many years an open market selling soft drugs. Recent political pressure and police clamp downs have stopped this. (Visitors are advised to use caution in this area after dark.)

Waterfront Opera House

From Christiania, continue along Prinsessegade to Holmen, where Copenhagen's dramatic new **Opera House** dominates the former docklands site on the harbourfront. Designed by Danish architect Henning Larsen, the modernist Opera House is topped by a spectacular 'floating' roof. The enormous, airy foyer holds an elegant pre-show restaurant and looks like something out of *2001: A Space Odyssey*. A number of the Nordic region's most eminent artists have contributed to the interior décor, including Per Kirkeby, who created stunning bronze reliefs. The building has been donated to the Danish state by the A.P. Møller and Chastine Mc-Kinney Møller Foundation.

> **Whether or not you're able to see an opera or ballet production at the city's new Opera House, a guided tour round the building is recommended (Mon–Wed 10am–4pm; tel: 33 69 69 69; charge; <www.operaen.dk>). The harbour bus and bus 66 serve the site.**

Furnishings and décor at the Amagermuseet

OUTLYING SIGHTS

A number 350S bus from Rådhuspladsen will take you south to Amager island, first to the village of Magleby and then to the charming community of Dragør. As many of the shops in Dragør are open on Sunday in summer – when they are mostly closed in Copenhagen – this is a good day to take the trip.

Amagermuseet

In an old farmhouse on the village street in Magleby you'll find **Amagermuseet** (Amager Museum; open May–Sept Tues–Sun noon–4pm; Oct–Apr Sun noon–4pm; admission fee; <www.amagermuseet.dk>). The kitchen and bedrooms are furnished in the old style with items donated by local residents representing a strong Dutch connection in the area. Christian II (1513–23) invited a colony of Netherlands farmers to improve soil cultivation in the region, and to provide the royal table with 'as many roots and onions as are needed'.

He gave the Dutch special privileges to live in Store Magle-by, which for centuries was referred to as Hollænderbyen (Dutchmen's Town). They had their own judicial system and church, and developed a bizarre local costume.

Dragør

Take the 350S bus for the 2-km (1-mile) trip to the water's edge at **Dragør**, where the harbour is packed with small boats and the 18th-century village remains remarkably preserved. A walk among the half-timbered cottages with their postage-stamp-size gardens provides a vivid impression of what life was like two or more centuries ago. Beside the harbour, a 1682 fisherman's cottage, the oldest house in the town, has been converted into **Dragør Museum** (open May–Sept Tues–Sun noon–4pm; admission fee; <www.dragoermuseum.dk>). It is devoted to local seafaring history.

Calm waters in the harbour at Dragør

Arken

Søren Robert Lund was just 25 years old and a student when he won a competition to design **Arken** (open Tues–Sun 10am–5pm, Wed till 9pm; free; <www.arken. dk>), to house a museum of modern art on the waterfront at Køge Bugt, 20km (12 miles) south of Copenhagen. The building gives the impression of a ship nestling in the dunes. An eclectic mix of exhibitions is staged here throughout the year. To reach Arken,

Grundtvigs Kirke, an early 20th-century masterpiece

take the S-train to Ishøj (lines A or E) then bus number 128 to the museum.

Grundtvigs Kirke

A 25-minute journey from Rådhuspladsen on bus number 10 brings you to **Grundtvigs Kirke** (open late-Mar–late-Oct Mon–Sat 9am–4pm, Thur till 6pm, Sun noon–4pm; late-Oct–late-Mar Mon–Sat 9am–4pm, Thur till 6pm, Sun noon–1pm; free; <www.grundtvigskirke.dk>) in northwest Copenhagen. The church is a monument to N.F.S. Grundtvig (1783–1872), a renowned educationalist, austere parson and prolific hymn-writer. Built between 1921 and 1940, it is also a monument to early 20th-century Danish architecture. The church's design by Peder Jensen-Klint is simple but effective. Everything is in pale-yellow brick, from the 50m (160ft) tower to the altar. It's a fitting tribute to a man who composed 1,400 hymns, and worth a visit.

EXCURSIONS

In a country of 44,030 sq km (16,630 sq miles), nature has in-geniously divided Denmark into a land of more than 450 islands so that you are never more than 50km (30 miles) from the sea. Copenhageners have their own beach, woodlands and wide lake area, and it is easy to organise an excursion. Options include boat trips, windmill and water-mill sightings, a visit to a royal country castle and exploring traditional villages.

Open-Air Folk Museum and Lyngby Lake

At Kongevejen 100, Sorgenfri, 16km (10 miles) north of the city, is **Frilandsmuseet**, the intriguing Open-Air Folk Muse-um (open Apr–Sept Tues–Sun 10am–5pm; free; <www.nat mus.dk>; times may vary, so before setting out check with the Copenhagen tourist information office, *see page 125*). The museum is accessible by car along the A3 and A5 main roads, by bus number 184 from Nørreport terminus in town, or by S-train to Sorgenfri station (leaving every 20 minutes from Copenhagen Central Station). A more interesting route is on the same train, but with a change at Jægersborg station to the little one-coach train known as *Grisen* ('The Pig'). This will drop you at Fuglevad Station near the museum's back entrance.

Forty farmhouses, cottages, workshops and a Dutch-type windmill are scattered about the 35-hectare (90-acre) site – all furnished in the original style, even down to combs and por-traits. Broadly, the buildings are split into geographical groups laid out along country lanes, together with bridges and village pumps, and all are authentically landscaped. Each building has been transplanted, tile by tile, timber by timber, from its original location. You'll find a Zealand group, a Jutland and a Faroes group, etc. Homes of all classes are represented, from peasant to landowner, as well as artisan and farmer.

Houses from the past at Frilandsmuseet, the Open-Air Folk Museum

The smell of old timber and tar pervades the rooms. Geese and sheep are driven along the lanes. Displays of folk dancing, sheep shearing, threshing and weaving are given during the summer. There are horse-and-carriage rides and picnic spots in tree-lined meadows.

Allow yourself time during good weather to stroll a kilometre or so along the road towards **Lyngby**, where you can take a rural boat ride scarcely equalled in any capital city. On your left is the white-walled baroque castle, Sorgenfri Slot (closed to the public), built in the 18th-century by Lauridz de Thurah who also designed the spire of Vor Frelsers Kirke *(see page 64)*.

Proceed over Mølleåen (the Mill Stream). Follow the signs to the right for Lyngby Sø-Bådfarten ('Lyngby Lake Boat Trip') to find two venerable canopied boats at the quayside. These have plied the four lakes since the 1890s. A 45-minute cruise, either Lyngby–Frederiksdal or Lyngby–Sophienholm, gives you the chance to savour the tree-covered backwaters and reedy lakes. The boats operate from May to September or October, depending on the weather.

As you float by, you'll pass the 1803 mansion of Marienborg amid the trees, the official summer residence of Danish prime ministers. Further on is Frederiksdal, with its castle on a hill above. This former royal house has been lived in by the same family since 1740. An alternative trip will take you to Sophienholm Mansion (1805), now a community cultural arts centre. Outdoor café tables give an idyllic view over the waters of Bagsværd Sø.

Back on Lyngby quay, the 184 bus can take you directly back into town, or it's a short walk to Lyngby S-train station.

Louisiana Museum of Modern Art

Some 130km (80 miles) of sea views and castle turrets, beaches and rolling farmland is what you can expect if you set about touring northern Zealand.

The closest of these attractions to Copenhagen, just to the north of Humlebæk and easily accessible by train, is the **Louisiana Museum for Moderne Kunst** (Louisiana Museum of Modern Art; open daily 10am–5pm, Wed till 10pm; admission fee; <www.louisiana.dk>). The museum is housed in the mid-19th-century mansion of a thrice-married cheese merchant whose wives were all named Louise. Airy white-washed galleries built into the hillside form the backdrop to an extensive collection, including works by Picasso,

Sculpture at Louisiana

Warhol and Rauschenberg, COBRA artists such as Asger Jorn, and more recently, Per Kirkeby. A glazed corridor leads past a group of Giacometti figures to the excellent Museum Café and a terrace featuring metal mobiles by Alexander Calder. In the gardens, you can sit on the lawns dotted with sculptures and marvel at Henry Moore's colossal bronze women silhouetted against the waters of the Øresund. There is an excellent range of daily children's activities, too.

Kronborg, Frederik II's Renaissance castle

Helsingør

Further north along the coast, at the narrowest stretch of the Øresund, is Helsingør, also known as Elsinore. Easily reached by train from Central Station, here is an attraction that should not be missed. On leaving Helsingør station, the town's most famous landmark comes into view, **Kronborg Slot** (Kronborg Castle; open May–Sept daily 10.30am–5pm; Apr and Oct Tues–Sun 11am–4pm; Nov–Mar Tues–Sun 11am–3pm; admission fee; <www.kronborg.dk>). To reach it on foot from the station takes about 20 minutes.

Many people will be familiar with Kronborg as 'Hamlet's castle', made famous by the film version starring Laurence Olivier and Vivien Leigh. The castle was built between 1574 and 1585 at the command of Frederik II for the purpose of extracting tolls from ships entering the narrow strait, and thus the Baltic. Frederik had more than just a stronghold in mind. He built a castle that could be lived in, fortified with ramparts and bastions so that a number of large windows and decorated towers could be added with impunity. He sent for the Flemish architect Antonius van Opbergen to design the four-wing structure, then engaged various Danish and Dutch artists to paint, weave and indulge in decorative sculpture on a scale never before seen in Scandinavia.

The moated brick castle today stands as Frederik's proudest memorial, now sparsely furnished but immensely impressive.

Mythical hero: Holger the Dane at Kronborg Slot

It has a feeling of solid strength and royal presence throughout, permeating the elaborate little chapel, the long galleries and stone stairways, and most of all the massive oak-beamed Great Hall. At 64 x 11m (210 x 36ft), it is the largest hall of its kind in northern Europe and one of the noblest rooms of the Danish Renaissance. Decked out now with 12 paintings of the Øresund by Isaac Isaacsz, its walls were once hung with 40 tapestries by the Dutchman Hans Knieper, depicting the 113 Danish kings said to have reigned before Frederik II. Fourteen of the tapestries survive, of which seven are to be seen in a small room beneath the hall, and the remainder are in the National Museum in Copenhagen *(see page 44)*. Underneath the castle are extensive cellars and dungeons, but the most renowned exhibit at Kronborg is the statue of the nation's own mythical hero, Holger the Dane. Legend has it that this 9th-century Viking warrior never actually died, but just went to sleep, waking in a time of trouble, or whenever Denmark was threatened, to help fight the country's enemies. During World War II, a section of the Resistance adopted the name of Holger Danske.

> **In Kronborg's northern wing, the Handels-og Søfartsmuseet (Trade and Maritime Museum) has an interesting collection of nautical paraphernalia, model ships and relics from early Danish settlements in Greenland and elsewhere.**

Helsingør has more to offer than the castle alone: there are medieval streets of colour-washed houses, the 15th-century **Skt Mariæ Kirke** and a **Carmelite Kloster** (Convent) to see. A short ferry trip across the strait to the colourful Helsingborg, Sweden, is always of interest.

If you visit Helsingør on Saturday, you will come face-to-face with a social phenomenon: Swedes by the thousands making the crossing to enjoy cut-price shopping in Denmark. High on their list is alcohol, their own laws being strict and the prices much steeper, and the shopkeepers of Helsingør are more than happy to oblige. As a consequence, stores selling spirits, wine and beer are prevalent, and it is a strange sight to see Swedes pushing around little two-wheeled trolleys with two cases of empty beer bottles. The number of cases is significant, as that is their duty-free limit, and the empty bottles will be replaced by full ones just before they embark for the sailing home.

Visits to Helsingør and to the Louisiana Museum of Modern Art may be readily combined. From Helsingør, board the

Rungstedlund, midway along the coast between the city and Helsingør, was home to *Out of Africa* author Karen Blixen. The house is now a museum devoted to her eventful life (www.karen-blixen.dk).

train for Copenhagen. Alight at Humlebaek; turn left on leaving the station and a 15-minute walk leads to the Louisiana museum. Alternatively, at the bus terminal next to the railway station in Helsingør board a number 388 bus for the pleasant 20-minute journey along the coast to the museum. To return to Copenhagen from Louisiana turn left onto the main road to walk back to Humlebæk railway station, or you can catch a bus.

Hillerød

Although Hillerød is just 9km (5 miles) from Helsingør and it is possible to visit both places in the same day, it is not really recommended as time and train timetable constraints combine against such a trip. You can reach the town by S-train from Copenhagen. Bus numbers 701 or 702 go from the station to the castle.

Hillerød is the site of Denmark's architectural showpiece, Christian IV's grandest achievement, and one of the greatest Renaissance castles in northern Europe, **Frederiksborg Slot** (Frederiksborg Castle; National History Museum open daily Apr–Oct 10am–5pm; Nov–Mar 11am–3pm; admission fee; <www.frederiksborgmuseet.dk>; gardens open daily 10am, closing at different hours depending on the season). This picturesque brick and sandstone castle is dramatically situated across three islands on a lake, and the best way to reach it is by way of a small boat that departs from the city centre. Although the oldest parts of the castle date from around 1560 and were built by Frederik II, most of the castle dates from between 1600 and 1620, his son,

Christian IV's, era. The style is Dutch Renaissance, and the result is spectacular. Danish monarchs resided here for about a century, and the absolute monarchs were crowned in the palace chapel from 1671.

In 1859 much of the interior was destroyed by fire, but between 1860 and 1884 it was rebuilt with financial support from the brewer J.C. Jacobsen and later the Carlsberg Foundation. Since 1878 the castle has been the home of the **Danmarks Nationalhistoriske Museum** (National History Museum). This occupies more than 60 rooms and contains a complete record of the Danish monarchy, beginning with Christian I, who established the Oldenburg line (1448–1863), through all the monarchs of the following Glücksburg line to the present queen, Margrethe II. Although the exhibits are of interest, the rooms of the castle are more so. Riddersalen (the Knights' Hall) and the chapel are Frederiksborg's ultimate

Frederiksborg Slot, home to Danish monarchs for 200 years

triumph. The 55-m (185-ft) Knights' Hall is awesome in its dimensions, with richly decorated tapestried walls, marble floor and carved wooden ceiling, all reconstructed from old drawings after the 1859 fire.

Below the Knights' Hall, Slotskirken (the chapel) escaped the fire, leaving its stunning gilt pillars and high vaulted nave virtually untouched. Almost every inch here is richly carved and ornamented. The chapel has inset black marble panels with quotations from the scriptures, marquetry panels in ebony and rare woods, and both its altar and pulpit in ebony with biblical scenes in silver relief. The organ is one of Europe's most notable, an almost unchanged original from 1610 by the Flemish master Esaias Compenius.

Around the gallery of this chapel hang the coats of arms belonging to knights of both the orders of the Elephant and the Grand Cross of Danneborg. Some modern recipients are also represented, such as Sir Winston Churchill and General Eisenhower.

Across the Øresund to Malmö

The opening in 2000 of the 8-km (5-mile) long Øresund Bridge linking Denmark and Sweden has brought economic benefits to the communities on either side of the water and made the possibility of an excursion to Malmö all the more appealing. Founded in the mid-13th century, Malmö is Sweden's third-largest city. It has an attractive old town surrounding Stortorget, the main square. The Tourist Information Office (tel: 46 40 34 12 00; <www.malmo.se>) at Malmö Central Station can supply maps and suggestions for walking routes and sells the Malmö Card, which includes a free sightseeing tour, free local bus travel and entrance to the castle and museums. Trains leave Copenhagen Central Station every 20 minutes from 5.20am to 12.40am. The journey takes 35 minutes.

Roskilde

According to legend, the Viking king Roar founded the town of **Roskilde** around 600. Situated 30km (19 miles) to the west of Copenhagen, this neat little town has plenty to offer those who undertake the 25-minute train journey from the capital.

Once you arrive, head straight for the centre, towards the three green spires which dominate the flat landscape. This is Roskilde's splendid **Domkirke** (Cathedral; open Apr–Sept Mon–Sat 9am–4.45pm, Sun and holidays 12.30–4.45pm; Oct–Mar Tues–Sat 10am–3.45pm, Sun and holidays

Roskilde Cathedral, a UNESCO World Heritage Site

12.30–3.45pm; admission fee; <www.roskildedomkirke.dk>).

One of the most remarkable buildings in Denmark, it began life as a wooden church built by King Harald Bluetooth around AD1000, when he first converted to Christianity. In the 1170s, Bishop Absalon, founder of Copenhagen *(see page 12)*, built a brick-and-stone cathedral here for his new bishopric, and during the course of the next 300 years this grew into the Romanesque-Gothic amalgam of today.

Christian IV added the distinctive spires in 1635. He also erected his own burial chapel and a gilded royal pew in the north wall of the church, heavily latticed and shielded from public view so that (it is said) he could smoke his pipe in

A chapel fit for a king at Roskilde Cathedral

peace during Sunday services. Nearly all the Danish kings and queens since Margrete I (who died in 1412) are buried in sarcophagi and chapels all different from one another in a jumbled symphony of style.

On the south side, the chapel of King Frederik V is a simple design in white paint and Norwegian marble, with 12 tombs grouped around it. In contrast, the Christian IV chapel on the north side is marked by elaborately wrought ironwork from 1618 and interior decoration mainly from the 19th century featuring frescoes, paintings depicting scenes from his reign, and bronze statues.

A light note is introduced by the clock high on the southwest wall of the nave: as each hour arrives, St George and his horse rear up, beneath them a dragon utters a shrill cry, a woman figure strikes her little bell four times with a hammer and a man rings his big bell once. The chapel on the outside of the cathedral beside the northwestern tower was inaugurated in 1985 and dedicated to the memory of Frederik IX, the King of Denmark from 1947–72, who is buried here.

To the front of the church is Stændertorvet, the traditional square of this old market town, lined with outdoor café tables in good weather, and fruit and vegetable stalls every Wednesday and Saturday morning. On Saturday there is also a popular flea market.

To the rear is parkland, where you can walk downhill through the meadow, towards the fjord and the **Vikingeskibshallen** (Viking Ship Museum; open daily 10am–5pm; admission fee; <www.vikingeskibsmuseet.dk>). When 11th-century Danes wanted to block off the sea route to Roskilde from the marauding Norwegians, they sank five Viking ships across a narrow neck of the shallow fjord here. These ships, salvaged in 1962, now form the basis of the museum and are superbly displayed. They include a warship of the type portrayed in the Bayeaux Tapestry and an awe-inspiring longship, the dreaded man o'war, used for long-range raiding.

The museum building stands on the edge of the water with one side made completely of glass, bringing the fjord almost into its main room. The outline of each ship was first reconstructed in metal strips, then the thousands of pieces of wood were treated and placed in position. The museum is lavishly illustrated with photographs and charts, and free film shows (in English) recount the full story of the salvage.

Salvaged ship in the Vikingeskibshallen

In recent years the Vikingeskibshallen has been developed into a fascinating complex in which you can see wooden boats being built by hand using the original skills, sail on one of these vessels, and eat in the attractive restaurant.

Then, to end the day in a truly Viking flavour, you can sample a draught of the favourite brew of these hardy sailors, *mjød* (mead).

WHAT TO DO

SHOPPING

Shopping in Copenhagen is a quality experience, and the city's pedestrian precincts and attractive squares add to the pleasure of seeking out those special purchases. A host of interesting shops in the pleasant side streets and arcades around the Strøget area specialise in everything from antiques to avant-garde furniture, while established department stores such as Illum and Magasin du Nord offer the very best in Danish design.

Shopping Hours

Shops are generally open Monday–Friday 9am or 10am–5.30pm or 7pm, and from 9am–1pm or 2pm on Saturday. However, shopping hours have been legally extended permitting stores to open from 6am–8pm if they so choose. A small number of shops (often food shops) are closed on Monday or Tuesday.

Certain stores stay open longer. These include bakers, florists, *smørrebrød* shops and kiosks. In addition, late-night (until 10pm or midnight) and Sunday shopping is possible at Central Station, which is like a village with a supermarket, banks open for foreign exchange, a post office, room-reservation service and snack bars.

Where to Shop

Undoubtedly the place to begin is Strøget (pronounced stroy-et), a charming pedestrian-only combination of four streets starting at Rådhuspladsen with Frederiksberggade, which leads into Nygade Vimmelskaftet, Amagertorv, Øster-

Interior space at the new Opera House

Magasin du Nord

gade, and ends in Kongens Nytorv square. Along Strøget, said to be the longest pedestrian-only street in the world, you will find everything you could possibly want, and much more. The finest ceramics, silver and crystal shops, superb home furnishings and interiors stores, the city's leading furriers, antiques shops, department stores, clothing shops and souvenir outlets exist harmoniously, side-by-side with a varied selection of restaurants and bars.

In the smaller streets branching off (and parallel to) Strøget are an eclectic array of music stores, potters and silversmiths, numerous antiques shops, and many designer fashion boutiques. On the opposite side of Kongens Nytorv, and convenient for those visiting Amalienborg and the Marble Church, are Bredgade and Store Kongensgade, with boutiques, galleries and more antiques shops.

Look out for a copy of the booklet *Funshopping København*. It will point you in the right direction for nearly 300 shops, restaurants, bars and hotels that you might otherwise miss. VAT, or sales tax (in Danish MOMS), is 25 percent on all products and services. Foreign visitors who make large purchases (minimum 300kr in any one store) in outlets that display 'Tax-Free Shopping' stickers will be given a form to reclaim the tax when they leave the country. Ask for details in the shop, *see page 121*, or check out the website <www.globalrefund.com>.

Good Buys

Royal Copenhagen (<www.royalcopenhagen.com>) is the collective name for a group of upmarket shops located in attractive historic buildings in the heart of Strøget at numbers 4, 6, 8 and 10 Amagertorv. These are the department store Illums Bolighus for the ultimate in modern design, home furnishings and accessories; Georg Jensen Silver; Royal Copenhagen Crystal; Royal Copenhagen Antiques and Georg Jensen Museum; and Royal Copenhagen Porcelain. The last of these, founded in 1775, is world-famous for its porcelain. The secret of its poetic effect is an underglaze technique that allows landscape pastels, and even accurate skin colours, to be reproduced. Blue motifs come out particularly well. All the pieces are hand-painted after a quick first firing, then fired again for glazing at 1,400°C (2,600°F). No two pieces are alike.

A hand-painted piece by Royal Copenhagen Porcelain

Also of interest is the Royal Copenhagen factory at Søndre Fasanvej 5, Frederiksberg – just a short bus ride from the city centre – where you can visit the workshops and see porcelain being painted, as well as purchase products from the factory shop.

Amber jewellery is offered everywhere, particularly in stores along Strøget. The local 'gem' (actually a fossil resin from the southern Baltic) may be cheaper here than at home, but beware, the quality can vary tremendously. Visit the House of Amber at Ravhuset, Kongens Nytorv 2.

Antiques are in plentiful supply, especially the homespun rather than the fine-art variety. The locals flock to Bredgade, off Kongens Nytorv, and Ravnsborggade (<www.ravnsborg gade.dk>), in the Nørrebro neighbourhood, which has more than 30 antiques shops.

Aquavit *(akvavit)*, the local spirit, usually flavoured with caraway seed, is cheaper than imported spirits. You'll find good prices at the airport duty-free store.

Crystal glassware and porcelain products are especially good buys if you want top-quality design matched with excellent craftsmanship. All the latest glass designs from Holmegaard – a glassworks just outside Copenhagen – are available from the company's main shop on Strøget (Amagertorv 8, <www.holmegaard.com>).

Down comforters. Once used, Danish comforters will not easily be forgotten. Ofelia, Amagertorv 3 (opposite the Royal Copenhagen complex on Strøget) has a wide range of comforters and duvets, as well as other products such as down slippers, which will keep your feet cosy throughout the winter months.

Check out the comprehensive shopping guides on <www.aok.dk> for an insider's guide to some of Copenhagen's best shopping quarters.

Furnishings. Danish furniture ranks among the world's best. Here you'll see items credited to the designer rather than to the factory. Furniture is a national pride

A new perspective on household items at Illums Bolighus

and most good pieces will have a black circular 'Danish Furniture-Makers' sticker attached. Lamps are also lovingly designed, as are household textiles and hand-woven rugs. The best stores for interior furnishings are: Illums Bolighus, Strøget, <www.royalshopping.com>, and Casa, Store Regnegade 2, <www.casagroup.com>.

Knitwear comes Nordic-style, often highly patterned, warm, and, in some cases, expensive. There are knitwear shops all over the city; some sell wool and patterns for those who are tempted to set about knitting their own garments, but the Sweater Market, Nytorv 19, off Strøget, just a few minutes from Rådhuspladsen, claims to be Europe's largest sweater store.

Stainless-steel household products. Danish and other Scandinavian knives and tableware are of the highest standard and Zwilling J.A. Henckels A/S, Vimmelskaftet 47, has by far the widest and most interesting array.

Stereo equipment. The very latest in stereo systems, CD players, radios, and TV sets can be found at the Bang & Olufsen Centre, Østergade 3–5, near Kongens Nytorv.

Silver is another Danish speciality, dominated by the name Georg Jensen. Silver in Denmark is quality-controlled and should always be hallmarked. The Jensen showrooms at Amagertorv 4 offer creations that range from key rings to highly precious jewellery.

Souvenirs are myriad. Little mermaid figures, Copenhagen dolls in frilly skirts and black lace caps, blue ceramic figurines and animals, and countless trolls and Vikings abound, as well as hand-painted spoons, racks and pepper mills. A particularly attractive Danish keepsake is an Amager shelf – a group of three or four small hand-painted shelves in a triangular frame that hangs on the wall. Beware, however, of cheap versions.

Danish glassware at the Holmegaard shop on Strøget

Toys are simple and attractive, especially those in solid wood. You'll also see hundreds of the Danish wooden soldiers in all sizes. Many stores such as Krea (Vestergade 4–6) have opened up, which specialise in educational toys for children of all ages.

Clocks and watches. Gullacksen Ure, Frederiks-berggade 8 on Strøget, may not be the largest of such shops, but its owner is the third generation of an old watchmaking family. Besides a wide selection of Danish and international brand-name watches, clocks, barometers and hygrometers, look for the museum pieces on the walls. Of particular interest are the practical Jacob Jensen temperature stations.

ENTERTAINMENT

When in Copenhagen, relax as the Danes do. Rent a bike for a different view of life, walk in the beech woods and parks, have a night on the town at a concert or jazz club – or simply pause for a snack on one of the many public benches.

Botanical Gardens. Avid gardeners could happily pass two or three days examining the 70 formal areas, the palm house and various other greenhouses on the 10-hectare (24-acre) Botanisk Have site opposite Rosenborg Castle, <www.botanic-garden.ku.dk>. It opens daily until sunset all year. Get there by bus 6A from Rådhuspladsen.

Café society. Another way of life altogether – relaxed and very welcoming. Sit as long as you like over a beer or coffee, gaze at the eccentric décor, and take time out to meet the Danes. There are several especially friendly bars in the area around the university.

Cycling. Some hotels lend bicycles to their guests at no charge. Otherwise they're easy to hire *(see page 108)*. You can use the extensive network of cycle paths *(cykelsti)* without any worry about cars, or indeed the weather – if it starts raining, country buses and trains will carry your bike and taxis have bicycle racks.

Nightlife

Classical music, opera, ballet. Scores of concerts are held throughout the year at the Royal Theatre, Tivoli, the Royal Conservatory of Music, Radio House, in churches and museums. Opera and ballet are performed at the splendid new Opera House – a small number of tickets are held back for sale on the day. The Royal Danish Ballet is internationally acclaimed, and rightly so – it is one of Europe's oldest with a repertory going back 200 years. Nowadays, the company experiments in modern dance as well, but its great tradition lies in Bournonville classics, such as *La Sylphide* and *The Dancing School*. The company performs from September to June.

Jazz, folk, rock. Copenhagen is one of Europe's leading jazz centres. The Copenhagen JazzHouse (Niels Hemmingsens Gade 10, <www.jazzhouse.dk>) is one of the city's premiere venues, hosting international, national and local artists. Mojo

The grand interior of the Royal Theatre, built in 1874

Blues Bar (Løngangstræde 21C, <www.mojo.dk>, is another great live music venue that is usually packed to the brim. There are several venues for folk music near the university, and an annual two-week Jazz Festival is held at the beginning of July.

> **If you are fortunate to be invited to a Danish home, don't turn down the opportunity. The Danes love to entertain and set great store by creating a cosy yet chic atmosphere for guests.**

One of the main venues for local and international rock and pop concerts is Amager Bio (Øresundsvej 6, <www.amager bio.dk>. Loppen in Christiania (<www.loppen.dk>) attracts a more artistic clientele, who come to see great local experimental, alternative, hardcore, world, jazz and rock shows. On summer Sundays free rock concerts are held in Fælled Park.

Nightclubs. Vega in Vesterbro (Enghavevej 40, <www.vega.dk>) is one of the city's biggest and best clubs, boasting two main rooms, as well as the retro Ideal Bar. Stereo Bar (Linnésgade 16A, <www.stereobar.dk>) is a local institution. Rust in Nørrebro (Guldbergsgade 8, <www.rust.dk>) is an intimate, laid-back nightclub with a minimalist, sci-fi atmosphere that hosts top DJs and has great live shows.

Cinemas. Close to Rådhuspladsen, Palads (Axeltorv 9), the Imperial (Ved Vesterport 4) and Dagmar Teatret (Jernbanegade 2) show mainstream blockbusters, and Grand Teatret (Mikkel Bryggers Gade 8) shows arthouse films. Most films are shown in their original language with Danish subtitles.

Casino. Casino Copenhagen, Radisson Hotel, 70 Amager Boulevard; tel: 33 96 59 96; <www.casinocopenhagen.dk>.

SPORTS

There are plenty of sporting activities to suit every taste within easy reach of the city. The top spectator sport is football (soccer), while popular participation sports include sailing and fishing. Ask the nearest Danish tourist office *(see page 125)* for an up-to-date list of what's available.

Fishing. Jutland is the Danish sea-fishing mecca, but you can still go for Øresund cod, mackerel, gar-pike, or flat-fish from Amager and the coast to the north of the city. A fishing licence costs 125kr (less for daily/weekly rates) and is available at any post office. You can rent licensed boats on Lyngby, Furesø and Bagsværd lakes on the northwest edge of Copenhagen.

Football. The Danish football team competes at the highest level, and the sport has an enthusiastic following. The main Copenhagen stadium is at Parken <www.parken.dk>, and is often used for major international matches.

Horse racing. The racetrack *(Galopbane)* at Klampenborg <www.galopbane.dk> is open mainly on Saturdays from mid-April–mid-December. To get there, take the S-train to Klampenborg, then catch either bus number 169 or 14.

Sailing. Join enthusiasts sailing on the Øresund and inland lakes. Yachts and cruisers are available for hire. Evidence of navigational proficiency is required for sailing on the Øresund, where a close watch must be kept for the constant ferry traffic. Book in advance with help from your local Danish tourist office *(see page 125)*.

Skating. Numerous stretches of water within the capital's boundaries freeze up in winter and outdoor rinks are set up in the city centre, such as at Frederiksberg Runddel. There are also indoor rinks *(skøjtehal)* at Copenhagen Forum and other suburban locations (open Oct–Apr)

Swimming. There is good sea bathing along the Zealand coast north and south of Copenhagen, but the sea is rarely warm. Nude bathing is mainly at Tisvildeleje, away from the north coast. There are about a dozen indoor swimming pools in Copenhagen, some with sauna/massage and gym facilities, and several outdoor pools which are open from mid-May until the end of August. So successful has the clean up of the Inner Harbour been that each bank is now home to an outdoor swimming pool. Havnefronten is on the south waterfront at Islands Brygge while Havneholmen is on the north waterfront near the Fisketorvet shopping complex (open Jun–Aug 11am–5pm).

Watersports. Water-skiing is popular on the Furesø, and it is possible to windsurf in Vedbæk harbour, tel: 45 89 12 23; contact Vedbæk Surfer Club, <www.v-surf.dk>, or consult the tourist office for details.

CHILDREN'S COPENHAGEN

Amusement parks. Tivoli *(see page 26)* should certainly appeal to the entire family. Less well known than Tivoli – and generally considered to be a rather downmarket version – is Bakken (tel: 39 63 35 44, <www.bakken.dk>), which is very popular with Danes. Situated on the outskirts of Klamp-

Football is Denmark's most popular spectator sport

enborg, just a 12-minute train ride from the city centre, it has approximately 100 rides, 35 cafés and restaurants and the country's most famous revue show. Entry is free.

Museums and attractions. Ripley's Believe it or Not Museum (Rådhuspladsen 57, tel: 33 32 31 31, <www.ripleys. dk>) houses a collection of 'bizarre but true' exhibits. Louis Tussaud's Wax Museum (HC Andersens Boulevard 22, tel: 33 11 89 00, <www.tussaud.dk>) has 200 wax effigies of celebrities and well-known figures. The Tycho Brahe Planetarium (Gammel Kongeve, tel: 33 12 12 24, <www.tycho.dk>) has 3D imax films and a great star show. The Experimentarium Science Centre (Tuborg Havnevej

Tycho Brahe Planetarium

7, tel: 39 27 33 33, <www. experimentarium.dk>) is a lively place where children are positively encouraged to tinker around with exhibits. At Christiansborg children can visit the Royal Stables *(see page 40)* and see the coaches and the horses that pull them.

Several major museums have special sections for children. These include the Nationalmuseet *(see page 44)*, Statens Museum for Kunst *(see page 61)* and the Louisana Museum *(see page 72)*. The Royal Danish Naval Museum (Orlogsmuseet; Overgaden Oven Vandet 58, tel: 33 11 60 37; <www.orlogsmuseet.dk>)

features a magnificent display of model ships, a children's playroom and a replica submarine into which kids can climb. The Viking Ship Museum at Roskilde *(see page 80)* has a children's section where two Viking ships may be boarded.

Entertainer at Bakken

Copenhagen's Zoologisk Have (Roskildevej 32, Frederiksberg, tel: 72 20 02 80, <www.zoo.dk>), established more than 120 years ago, is a good place to spend an afternoon. It houses more than 2,500 animals and has a fine children's section, restaurant and cafeteria. It's a 10-minute ride from Rådhuspladsen by bus 6A. Approximately 10km (6 miles) from the city centre, at Charlottenlund, is Danmarks Akvarium (tel: 39 62 32 83; <www.danmarksakvarium.dk>), which is best visited during feeding times.

Swimming. Indoors, the Vandkulturhuset (Water Culture House) at the DGI sports centre (Tietgensgade 65, tel: 33 29 81 40, <www.dgi-byen.dk>) is a state-of the-art swimming complex with facilities for children of all ages. Outdoors, the newly opened two Inner Harbour swimming pools *(see page 93)* have children's pools. Adjacent to the pool at Islands Brygge there is a skateboarding park.

Tours. Almost anything to do with water appeals to youngsters, and organised canal trips are a must *(see page 116)*. Also worth considering are boat cruises including a voyage aboard a Viking vessel that departs from Roskilde *(see page 80)* and cruises from Lyngby *(see page 71)*.

Calendar of Events

Most of Copenhagen's annual festivals involve music. For an up-to-the-minute guide to what's on, visit the Tourist Information Office *(see page 125)* or pick up a copy of *Copenhagen This Week* .

January Venue Rock Festival: underground rock on the last weekend.

Shrovetide Beating the Barrel, parades and carnival festivities, centred around Rådhuspladsen and the Nationalmuseet. Also at Dragør on Amager island.

April Queen's birthday (16 April): crowds gather outside Amalienborg Slot at noon for the Queen's balcony appearance.

May Day Marches and brass bands converge on Fælled Park.

Whitsuntide Copenhagen Carnival: colourful Latin-style processions attract large numbers of spectators.

June St Hans Eve Festival (23 June): bonfires are lit in Fælled Park and along the city's northern beaches to celebrate the longest day of the year. Roskilde Festival (end of June): the country's biggest rock festival.

July Copenhagen Jazz Festival: bands play every jazz style from bebop onwards, on stage, in pubs and on the streets. Copenhagen Historic Grand Prix: vintage cars take to the streets.

August Ballet Festival: performances by the Royal Danish Ballet. Copenhagen Summer Festival: chamber music at Charlottenborg. Golden Days in Copenhagen (August–September): recalls the Golden Age of the 19th century with plays, ballet and concerts, walking tours of the city and excursions (full programme of events from the Tourist Office). Glyptotekets Sommerkoncerter (mid-August–early September): classical music in Ny Carlsberg Glyptotek.

September Blues Festival: concerts at venues across the city.

October Night of Culture: museums, galleries, churches, libraries and theatres open their doors after dark and invite the public inside. Copenhagen's Gay and Lesbian Film Festival. Autumn Jazz Festival.

November–December Tivoli is transformed into a winter wonderland during illuminations, ice-skating and a Christmas market.

EATING OUT

Food is of a high standard in Denmark, and counts as little short of an obsession. Danes at home will happily spend two hours over their *frokost* (lunch) or up to four hours if entertaining special guests, while a *middag* (dinner) in celebratory mood can last from 6pm to very, very late.

Restaurants and Bars

There are more than 2,000 assorted restaurants, cafés, bars and snack bars in Copenhagen. Restaurants often serve a special dish of the day *(dagens ret)* and what is known as the *dan-menu* – a two-course Danish lunch or dinner for a fixed price – in addition to *à la carte* items. Keep an eye open for a *daglig kort* (daily menu), which usually features less-expensive dishes than those listed on the more formal menu *(spisekort)*. You'll also find little lunch-only, cosy cellar restaurants listed in *Copenhagen This Week (see page 120)*. These offer good value with an old-world charm, and are frequented by Danes themselves. Copenhagen has more than its fair share of fine restaurants, ten of which have been awarded

Alfresco dining on Nyhavn

a Michelin star. For a drink, drop into one of the numerous cafés, pubs or bars dotted throughout the city.

VAT and service charges are included in the bill. Danes are not tip-minded, although after a meal you may want to round up your bill. At very good restaurants, after excellent service, show your appreciation with up to a 5 percent tip.

Breakfast

Breakfast *(morgenmad)* in a Danish hotel is a far cry from the Spartan 'continental breakfast' of a roll and a cup of coffee. Bread rolls, cold cuts, cheeses, jam, pastries and probably eggs are all accompanied by milk and fruit juice followed by tea or coffee.

Cold Dishes

Cold food is Denmark's truly outstanding culinary speciality. *Smørrebrød* (open sandwiches) are thickly buttered slices of heavy Danish rye bread covered with one of a wide array of delicacies: liver pâté *(leverpostej)*, veal *(kalvekød)*, ham *(skinke)*, roast beef *(stegt oksekød)*, salmon *(laks)*, smoked eel *(røget ål)*, shrimp *(reje)*, cod roe *(torskerogn)*, pickled herring *(sild)*, a variety of salads *(salat)* or cheese *(ost)*. This main layer is garnished with various accessories that have been carefully chosen to enhance both taste and appearance.

Larger restaurants have scores of different *smørrebrød*. The usual procedure is to mark your orders on the menu itself, specifying which kind of bread you want *(knækbrød:* crispbread; *rugbrød:* rye; *franskbrød:* white; or *pumpernikkel:* black).

Don't confuse your *smørrebrød* with the Swedish word *smörgåsbord,* which has gained international currency as a description of the Scandinavian cold buffet-style spread, better known in Denmark as *det store kolde bord* (the cold

Copenhagen's restaurants offer a wide choice of seafood dishes

table). There can be a bewildering array of dishes. For a fixed price, you start at one end of the table, helping yourself to herring in various forms, seafood, salads and other delicacies, and go on to sample liver pâté, ham and other cuts of meat. Despite its name, the cold table always includes a few hot items, such as meatballs, pork sausages, soup and fried potatoes. Several kinds of bread and salads are also provided. Danish *akvavit (see page 103)* and beer go especially well with *koldt bord*.

Fish and Shellfish

Fish (or small canapés) is the traditional first course of a full meal. It is also available as a main course, and a great variety of fish appears on the Danish menu. Herring is one of the firm favourites, and may be served pickled or fried, with a sherry, vinegar, curry or fennel dressing. Succulent red Greenland shrimps are also popular. Lobster is also of-

> **A summer seafood speciality is *danske rejer*, small pink shrimps from local waters that are served piled high on white bread.**

fered – though it is not cheap – as is crab, cod and halibut. Plaice features frequently in the local cuisine and may be served boiled or fried with a garnish of shellfish or parsley. You'll see the Øresund *rødspætte* (red-spot plaice) on every menu.

One great Scandinavian delicacy is *gravad laks*, in which raw salmon is pressed with salt and a small amount of sugar, and then sprinkled generously with chopped dill. A creamy sauce of oil, mustard and sugar is traditionally served alongside as an accompaniment.

Meat and Poultry

Although Danish meat dishes most frequently make use of pork and veal, beef has made a major breakthrough, as Danish farmers now breed more cattle. The kinds of steak that you are most likely to be offered are *fransk bøf*, fillet steak served with herb butter and French fries, and *engelsk bøf*, fillet steak served with fried onions and potatoes.

The top restaurants cook in classic French/international style. In small establishments, some typical Danish hot dishes appear on the menu such as *mørbradbøf*, a delectable legacy of the pork-only days – small cuts of tenderloin, lean, very tasty and served as a main course with boiled potatoes, onions and gravy.

More ordinary fare – but delicious nevertheless – are Danish meatballs (*frikadeller*), a finely minced mixture of pork and veal, often served with potato salad and red cabbage. *Biksemad* is also cheap and tasty: a Danish hash of diced potatoes, meat and onions with a fried egg on top. A hearty Danish stew is *Hvids labskovs*, made from chunks of beef boiled with potatoes, peppercorns and bay leaves.

Chicken is most often served roasted with potatoes fried in butter and a cucumber salad *(agurkesalat)*. Roast duck is served with apple or prune stuffing and is usually accompanied by caramelised potatoes and a generous array of vegetables.

Salads

The word for salad, *salat*, has two meanings. It can be a side dish of fresh lettuce, tomato, sliced egg and plentiful red peppers; or, more often, it's one of several mayonnaise mixtures, which are eaten on *smørrebrød* or as an appetiser. *Italiensk salat* consists of carrots, asparagus, peas and macaroni. *Skinkesalat* is basically chopped ham; *sildesalat* comprises marinated or pickled herring, beetroot and apple. These are the most common of the many sandwich salads available.

Stalls filled with fresh produce in a city market

Cheese and Fruit

Danish Blue *(Danablue)*, a rich, sharp-flavoured cheese, has always had a strong international following, along with Havarti. Fynbo and Samsø, both relatively mild and firm cheeses, possess a sweet, almost nutty flavour. *Rygeost*, smoked cream cheese spiced with cumin seed, is wonderful.

Desserts

It will have been obvious from the time you arrived that Denmark is not a good place for dieting. And by the time you get to the desserts your best intentions will have been quite definitely routed. Your dessert will almost certainly be laced with cream *(fløde)* or whipped cream *(flødeskum)*.

Skål!

Favourite desserts include: *æblekage* (stewed apples with vanilla, served with alternating layers of biscuit crumbs and topped with whipped cream) and *bondepige med slør* (a mixture of rye-bread crumbs, stewed apple, sugar and the ubiquitous whipped cream).

Snacks

For a snack with a difference, try the deep-fried Camembert cheese served with toast and strawberry jam *(ristet franskbrød med friturestegt camembert og jordbærsyltetøj)*. The university area is good for cheap goulashes, hashes, chicken and *håndmadder* (usually three slender *smørrebrød* with different toppings). Hot-dog stands *(pølsevogn)* are found everywhere, serving red Danish sausages *(pølse)* with mustards and relishes.

Curiously, Danish pastry is known here as Viennese pastry *(wienerbrød)*. This distinctive light and flaky delight can be found in any *konditori* (bakery), and makes a delectable snack in the middle of the morning or afternoon.

Drinks

Golden Danish lager comes in several types: *lys pilsner* (light lager), which has only 2 percent alcohol; the more normal green-bottle pilsner; and the stouts and special beers (such as Carlsberg Elephant) at 6 to 7 percent or more. Pilsner is available everywhere almost 24-hours a day. In addition, more diverse beers have become available recently, with excellent microbrews and imported European beers widely sold.

Akvavit is fiery Danish schnapps made from potatoes, often with a caraway taste. The colour varies according to the herbs and spices that have been used for flavouring. It is sipped at

---

Skål! ...and tak!

Learn to say *skål* (the vowel is between 'loll' and 'hall') with your beer or akvavit. It's more than just Danish for 'cheers', it's a ritual if you are invited to a Danish home. Your host usually has the privilege of making the first toast, and will raise a glass, point it towards everyone in turn, looking directly at them, and say *'skål!'*. After all have taken a sip or a swallow, the host will look at each again in turn before putting down the glass.

After the meal itself, the appropriate – and essential – words to say are *'tak for mad'* (pronounced 'tak for maad'), meaning, very simply, 'thanks for the meal'.

mealtimes during the opening fish course or with the cheese, and will sometimes be washed down with a beer chaser. If you order *akvavit* with your meal, the bottle may occasionally be put on the table for you to help yourself. Don't be deluded into thinking you'll only be charged for a single measure – back in the bar they'll know exactly how much has gone.

All wines are imported and while there is a wide selection of French, German and Italian varieties, they are always rather expensive in restaurants. Even cheap house wine *(husets vin)* may be three times the supermarket price. After your dinner, try the Danish cherry liqueur, *Cherry Heering*.

Coffee *(kaffe)* can be found everywhere – rich, strong, and served with cream. The price may seem high, but the waiter will usually come around offering refills. On a chilly day you might like to try *varm kakao med flødeskum* – a hot cocoa with whipped cream.

Carlsberg, brewed in the capital

To Help You Order ...

Could we have a table?   **Kan vi få et bord?**

Do you have a set menu?   **Har De en fast menu?**

I'd like a/an/some ...   **Jeg vil gerne have ...**

beer	**en øl**	napkin	**en serviet**
bread	**brød**	pepper	**peber**
coffee	**kaffe**	potatoes	**kartofler**
dessert	**en dessert**	salad	**en salat**
fish	**fisk**	salt	**salt**
glass	**et glas**	soup	**suppe**
ice cream	**is**	sugar	**sukker**
meat	**kød**	tea	**te**
menu	**et spisekort**	vegetables	**grønsager**
milk	**mælk**	(iced) water	**(is) vand**
mustard	**sennep**	wine	**vin**

...and Read the Menu

agurkesalat	cucumber salad	**lagkage**	layer cake
blomkål	cauliflower	**lever**	liver
citron	lemon	**løg**	onion
flæskesteg	roast pork and crackling	**medisterpølse**	pork sausage
grøn peber	green pepper	**nyre**	kidney
grønne bønner	French beans	**oksekød**	beef
gulerødder	carrots	**pommes frites**	French fries
hamburgerryg	loin of pork		
hindbær	raspberry	**porre**	leek
jordbær	strawberry	**rødkål**	red cabbage
kartoffelmos	mashed potatoes	**ssvinekød**	pork
kirsebær	cherry	**øtunge**	sole
kotelet	chop	**æble**	apple
kylling	chicken	**æg**	egg
kål	cabbage	**æggekage**	omelette

HANDY TRAVEL TIPS

An A–Z Summary of Practical Information

A

ACCOMMODATION *(hotel; indlogering)* See also CAMPING, YOUTH HOSTELS and RECOMMENDED HOTELS on page 127

Since 1997 all hotels that are members of the Association of the Hotel, Restaurant, and Tourism Industry in Denmark (HORESTA) have been classified on a scale of one to five stars, based on objective criteria. Rates on *page 127* are averages for double rooms in high season, service charges and taxes included, but these can be down by as much as 50 percent at other times of the year. You will find that a hearty Danish breakfast is usually included in the rate.

A *Hotel Guide* is available from any Danish Tourist Board office.

The Copenhagen Tourist Information (4a Vesterbrogade, tel: 70 22 24 42, fax: 70 22 24 52,<www.visitcopenhagen.com>; *see page 125*) is across the street from Central Station and can assist you with accommodation either before you leave home, or upon arrival in Copenhagen.

How much is a room for one person/two people? Is breakfast included?	**Hvad koster et enkeltværelse/ dobbeltværelse? Er der morgenmad?**

AIRPORT *(lufthavn)*

Copenhagen Airport, Kastrup, (<www.cph.dk>), around 10km (6 miles) from the city centre, is considered to be the main northern European hub, and is one of the continent's busiest airports.

The quickest way to Copenhagen city centre – Central Station – is on the fast train link that leaves from track 2 (located under Terminal 3) three times every hour, takes just 12 minutes and costs around 25kr. The airport bus runs from the airport every 15 minutes and takes 25 minutes to Central Station. The regular bus, 250S, departs from outside Terminal 3 every 15 minutes between 5.30am–midnight and takes 35 minutes.

Taxis take between 20–30 minutes; expect to pay 150–250kr.

B

BICYCLE HIRE *(cykeludlejning)*

The City Bike Foundation (tel: 32 54 00 79; <www.bycyklen.dk>) has 2,500 free city bikes at racks throughout the city centre. Simply take one out by putting 20kr into the slot. Remember, though, you can only use it within the limits shown – you are subject to a 1,000kr fine if stopped by police outside City Bike Country – and when you return it to a City Bike rack you get your 20kr back. It is much better to rent a decent bike from one of the many bike shops. This costs about 70kr per day for a three-speeder. Bikes can be put on S-tog trains except during rush hours. Look for carriages with a cycle symbol.

BUDGETING FOR YOUR TRIP

The following are some average prices in Danish kroner (kr) for basic expenses. However, remember that all prices must be regarded as approximate. Danes round off the bill, up or down, to the closest amount possible divisible by 25 øre because there are no intermediate coins (eg, 13 is rounded off to 25).

Car rental. Fiat Punto approx. 700kr per day, 2,700kr per week; Volvo S60 1,600kr per day, 4,800kr per week; VW Passat Wagon 1,200kr per day, 3,500kr per week; all prices include collision damage waiver and local taxes.

Entertainment. Cinema 60–80kr; Royal Danish Opera tickets 70–450kr; nightclub entry 50–110kr; Tivoli Gardens: adults 75kr, children 35kr.

Hotels. 5-star 2,500kr; 4-star 1,600kr; 3-star 1,200kr; 2-star 800kr; 1-star 600kr. These are average rates which include breakfast, VAT and service.

Meals and drinks (at a fairly good establishment). Lunch 100kr, dinner 150–350kr, sandwich *(smørrebrød)* 20–30kr, coffee 15kr, *akvavit* (schnapps) 30kr, beer 40kr, soft drink 25kr.

Public transport. Single ride on the bus, S-train or Metro costs 19kr and up. Many travellers buy a 24-hour ticket for 110kr (children 55kr), or better yet, a Copenhagen Card *(see page 125)*, which includes transport and admission to attractions.

Taxi. The basic fare is 23kr *(see page 124)*.

C

CAMPING

There are more than 500 approved camp sites in Denmark for tents, caravans and camper vans. Several also have cabins for rent. These are inspected annually and classified with a one- to five-star rating. All the 2- to 5-star sites have facilities for motor homes. You must obtain a Camping Pass valid for one calendar year and these are available at any camp-site office for 80kr for an individual, or for a couple, or for a family (comprising children under 18 years old). A pass for a single overnight stay costs 20kr. No camping is permitted outside official sites.

You can pick up a comprehensive free brochure on camping, youth hostels and student hotels from the Danish Tourist Board in your country *(see page 126)*. Alternatively, for general information on camping in Denmark and sites in and around Copenhagen, contact Campingrådet, Mosedalsvej 15, 2500 Valby; tel: 39 27 88 44; fax 38 27 80 44; <www.campingraadet.dk>.

Can we camp here?	**Må vi campere her?**

CAR HIRE *(biludlejning)* See also DRIVING AND BUDGETING FOR YOUR TRIP

In reality, visitors to Copenhagen and the numerous attractions in its immediate vicinity will find that having a car is more of a hindrance than an assistance, especially because the public-transport system is superb. Car rental, like fuel, is not inexpensive and traffic offences such as drink-driving have severe penalties.

If you decide to rent once you are in Copenhagen, then contact Avis, tel: 33 26 80 00, <www.avis.dk>; Europcar, tel: 70 11 66 99, <www.europcar.dk>; Hertz, tel: 33 17 90 90, <www.hertzdk.dk>; or Budget, tel: 33 55 05 00, <www.budget.dk>

To rent a car, you will need a valid national (or international) driving licence and be at least 20 years of age (25 for some companies). Most agencies will require payment by credit card.

CLIMATE AND CLOTHING

Climate. Denmark's relatively temperate climate is due to its situation and the sea currents, but frequent switches in the wind also bring changeable weather. Spring may come late, but summer is often sunny and autumn mild. Average monthly temperatures in Copenhagen are:

	J	F	M	A	M	J	J	A	S	O	N	D
°C	0.5	0	2	6	11	16	17	16	13	9	5	2
°F	33	32	35	42	52	60	63	61	56	48	40	36

Clothing. Casual clothes are suitable for nearly every occasion, including the theatre and most dining out. Only in top-class hotels, restaurants and clubs – and even then not uniformly – will men be required to wear a tie in the evening, and here women will not look out of place in something dressy. Otherwise, go as you like. Summer nights are long and light but often chilly, so a sweater or cardigan is essential. Bring a light overcoat or raincoat, in addition to ordinary summer clothes – the weather has an awkward habit of changing. On the beach, you can be as undressed as you like.

Spring and autumn have many hours of sunshine, but winter can be downright cold and damp, and you should pack plenty of warm clothes (plus a raincoat). In all seasons, comfortable walking shoes are highly recommended for your excursions on foot around town.

COMPLAINTS

The Danish sense of fair play makes complaining a rare event, and complaints themselves often unnecessary. In a restaurant or hotel, a quiet word with the manager is usually enough. Serious complaints about hotels or other services should be directed to the Copenhagen Tourist Office *(see page 125)* or to the appropriate travel authority.

CRIME AND SAFETY See also EMERGENCIES AND POLICE

Copenhagen is no longer among the safest capital cities in Europe. Pickpockets are rampant and petty crime is on the increase. Take normal precautions. Keep a close eye on your belongings. Hesitate before walking out alone in the very early hours through seedy areas – your hotel receptionist can give advice if you are in doubt about night-time locations that you wish to visit. It is also best to be very careful in the Christiania area, both by day and night.

It is a good policy to place your valuables – including passport and airline tickets – in the hotel safe. Another sensible precaution is to take photocopies of passports and airline tickets and keep them separate from the originals. In instances where the originals are stolen, lost or damaged, this will save an enormous amount of time and hassle with the authorities. Any loss or theft should be reported at once to the nearest police station, if only for insurance purposes; your insurance company will need to see a copy of the police report.

CUSTOMS AND ENTRY FORMALITIES *(told)*

Visitors from Britain and most countries outside the EU need a valid passport to enter Denmark; citizens from EU countries, excluding Britain, need only an identity card. You are generally entitled to stay in Denmark for up to three months without a visa (this period includes the total amount of time spent in Denmark, Finland, Iceland, Norway and Sweden in any six-month period.)

South African citizens will need a visa. Contact the Embassy of Denmark, Senlam Centre, 8th Floor, Pretorius/Andries Streets, Pretoria,

0002, South Africa, tel: (27) 012 322 0595; fax: (27) 012 322 0596. European and North American residents are not subject to any health requirements. In case of doubt, check with Danish representatives in your own country before departure.

Duty-free allowance. As Denmark is part of the European Union, free exchange of non-duty-free goods for personal use is permitted between Denmark and other EU countries. Due to the high prices of alcohol and tobacco visitors might consider bringing in some of their own. If so, each person over 20 is allowed 1 litre of liquor (over 22 percent by volume) and 200 cigarettes (or 50 cigars) if living in the EU, and 400 cigarettes if living outside the EU.

D

DRIVING

If you take your car into Denmark from the UK then you will need a valid driver's licence, car registration papers, a Green Card (an extension of your regular insurance policy, valid for travel abroad – though not obligatory for EU countries, it's still preferable to have it), a red warning triangle in case of breakdown and a national identity sticker for your car. British car-owners should note that left dipping headlights are illegal. Headlights are compulsory at all hours.

Driving conditions. Drive on the right, pass on the left. Traditionally, traffic coming from your right has priority, and clear indication should always be given when changing lanes. Weaving from one lane to another is a punishable offence.

Pedestrian crossings are sacrosanct and nearly always controlled by lights. Beware of buses pulling out from stops – you should give way to them. Use caution for cyclists and moped riders to your right, often on their own raised paths *(cykelsti)*, but sometimes divided from you merely by a white line, which you should not cross.

Seat belts must be worn by driver and passengers. Motorcycle, moped and scooter drivers, and their passengers, must wear helmets.

Speed limits. On the *motorvej* (motorway), the limit is 110km/h (68mph), rising to 130km/h (80 mph) in some places. On other roads it is 80km/h (50mph), and in built-up areas (indicated by white signs with town silhouettes) it drops to 50km/h (30mph). For cars with caravans it is 70km/h (45mph) outside built-up areas and 80km/h (50mph) on motorways. If you are caught speeding, there's a heavy, on-the-spot fine.

Drinking and driving. The law is stringent: if you are discovered to have more than 0.5 milligrams of alcohol per thousand litres in your blood while driving, you face severe penalties.

Road signs. International pictographs are in widespread use in Copenhagen, but below are translations of some local signs:

Blind vej	Dead-end road (cul-de-sac)
Fare	Danger
Fodgængere	Pedestrians
Indkørsel forbudt	No entry
Omkørsel	Diversion
Rabatten er blød	Soft shoulders
Udkørsel	Exit
Vejarbejde	Roadworks

E

ELECTRICITY

The supply for electrical appliances in Denmark is 220 volt, 50 Hz AC, and requires standard two-pin, round continental plugs. Visitors should bring their own adaptors.

EMBASSIES AND CONSULATES

The embassies, with consulate sections, are generally open Mon–Fri 8am–4pm, but there is usually a 24-hour telephone service. New Zealand does not have an embassy in Denmark.

Australia: embassy: Dampfærgevej 26, 2nd floor, DK-2100 Copenhagen Ø; tel/fax: 70 26 36 76.

Canada: embassy: Kristen Bernikowsgade 1, DK-1105 Copenhagen K; tel: 33 48 32 00; fax: 33 48 32 20.

Republic of Ireland: embassy: Østbanegade 21, DK-2100 Copenhagen Ø; tel: 35 42 32 33; fax: 35 43 18 58.

South Africa: embassy: Gammel Vartovvej 8, DK-2900 Hellerup; tel: 39 18 01 55; fax: 39 18 40 06

UK: embassy and consulate: Kastelsvej 36–40, DK-2100 Copenhagen Ø; tel: 35 44 52 00; fax: 35 44 52 93.

USA: embassy and consulate: Dag Hammarskjölds Allé 24, DK-2100 Copenhagen Ø; tel: 35 55 31 44; fax: 35 43 02 23.

EMERGENCIES see also POLICE and HEALTH AND MEDICAL CARE

The all-purpose emergency number is 112 and is free from public phone boxes. Ask for police, fire or ambulance. Speak distinctly (English will be understood) and state your number and location.

To speak with a doctor during the day, ask your hotel to help. After hours (4pm–8am) and weekends, call the on-call GP on 70 13 00 41.

Dental emergency. Tandlægevagten, Oslo Plads 14, is open Mon–Fri 8am–9.30pm, Sat–Sun and public holidays 10am–noon; tel: 35 38 02 51. Cash payment only.

Can I use your phone?	**Må jeg låne din telefon?**
I have lost my bag/	**Jeg har mistet min**
wallet.	**taske/tegnebog.**

G

GAY AND LESBIAN TRAVELLERS

Denmark has one of Europe's most liberal attitudes towards gays and lesbians, and this is reflected in its legislation. In common with most of Scandinavia, the age of consent is the same as for heterosexuals. Copenhagen has a thriving gay scene, and there are bars, clubs and a few hotels where gays are openly welcome. For information, contact the Landsforeningen for Bøsser og Lesbiske (National Association for Gays and Lesbians), Teglgårdstræde 13; tel: 33 13 19 48; <www.lbl.dk>.

GETTING TO COPENHAGEN

Air travel. The following airlines are among those operating regular services to Copenhagen **from the UK**: SAS (Scandinavian Airlines System; tel: 0870 6072 7727; <www.scandinavian.net>), Maersk Air (tel: 020 7333 0066; <www.maersk-air.com>), British Airways (tel: 0870 850 9850; <www.britishairways.com>), British Midland (tel: 0870 6070 555; <www.flybmi.com>), EasyJet (tel: 0905 821 0905; <www.easyjet.com>), Virgin Express (tel: 0870 7301 134; <www.virginexpress.com>).
From the USA and Canada: SAS (Scandinavian Airlines System), tel: 1-800-221-2350; <www.flysas.com>, operates daily flights to Copenhagen from Newark and Chicago.
From Australia and New Zealand: There are no direct flights from these countries. Depending upon the city of destination Qantas, the Australian national airline, operates in conjunction with other airlines. Flights to Copenhagen necessitate two, sometimes three, changes, usually in the Far East and then Europe. Air New Zealand operates flights from Auckland to London and then from London on BA to Copenhagen.

Rail travel. You can travel to Copenhagen by train from London Liverpool Street to Harwich, then by DFDS Seaways to Esbjerg and onwards by train to Copenhagen (tel: 08705 333 000; <www.dfdsseaways.dk>). Alternatively, you can take the Eurostar from London Waterloo International (due to move to London St Pancras in late 2007) to Brussels and a connecting service to Copenhagen (Rail Europe, tel: 08708 371 371; <www.raileurope.co.uk>).

Rail Passes. Rail Europe *(contact details above)*, offers a variety of rail passes that must be purchased before leaving home, and can be used in Denmark alone or in Denmark and other Scandinavian and/or European countries.

Coach travel. Contact Eurolines (tel: 0870 514 3219; <www.euro lines.co.uk>) for details of coach services from London to Copenhagen.

GUIDES AND TOURS *(guide)*

The Association of Authorised Guides offers individual and group tours. For reservations tel: 33 11 33 10, fax: 33 11 37 05, <www. guides.dk>. Open Mon 2–4pm, Tues and Thurs 10am–noon.

Canal and harbour tours. DFDS Canal tours (tel: 33 42 33 20; <www. canal-tours.dk>) and Netto Boats (tel: 32 54 41 02; <www.netto-baadene.dk>) run 50-minute guided canal tours from Apr–Oct between 10am and 5pm (until 7.30pm in July and Aug). The DFDS tours depart from Nyhavn and Gammel Strand; Netto tours depart from Holmens Church. DFDS also runs the 'hop-on-hop-off' harbour bus, with six stops at different attractions. Kayak Tours (tel: 40 50 40 06; <www. kajakole.dk>) depart from Gammel Strand for 1½–3hr canal voyages in kayaks equipped with intercom.

Brewery tours. A brewery visit is an excellent way to sample a free bottle or two, whilst also discovering how every glass you drink is a contribution to art, science or industry: Carlsberg donates vast sums through its charitable foundations. Carlsberg (tel: 33 27 13 14; <www. visitcarlsberg.com>) is near the famous Elephant Gate, Gamle Carlsbergvej 11 (bus 26 from Rådhuspladsen); open Tues–Sun 10am–4pm.

City tours. Copenhagen Excursions (tel: 32 54 06 06; <www.cex.dk>) and Auto Paaske/Vikingbus (tel: 32 66 00 00; <www.sightseeing.dk>) depart from in front of the Palace Hotel at Rådhuspladsen (City Hall Square) every 30 minutes from Apr–Oct on 'hop-on-hop-off' city tours. The same companies run extensive Grand Tours lasting 2½ hours. These depart throughout the year at 11am with additional departures daily mid-May–Sept at 1.30pm and Oct–mid-May Sat 1.30pm. These companies also run City & Harbour Tours, which last 2½ hours and depart from mid-May–Sept 9.30am, 11.30am and 1.30pm.

Copenhagen's cycle culture has extended to the introduction of trishaws. Companies that run city tours and taxi services using trishaws include Copenhagen Rickshaw (tel: 35 43 01 22; <www.rickshaw.dk>), and Cykeltaxi (tel: 70 26 00 55; <www.cykeltaxi.com>) which uses electrically-assisted pedal power. When used as taxis the flag-drop for these services is usually 25kr. Haggling is not inappropriate. Alternatively, City Safari (tel: 33 23 94 90; <www.citysafari.dk>) run guided bike tours of the city.

Industrial art tours. Guided tours in English of the Royal Copenhagen porcelain factory, Welcome Centre Søndre Fasanvej 5, tel: 38 14 92 97, Mon–Fri 9am–4pm. Similar tours are available for silver and glass works.

Trips to Sweden. Sweden is so close and accessible that it really is worth the short trip – if only to see how Swedes differ from Danes. Trains to Malmö over the Øresund Bridge take 35 minutes. An alternative is to combine a trip to Helsingør with the 20-minute ferry service to Helsingborg in Sweden. The more adventurous can try a 'Round the Sound' trip. Buy tickets from DSB (Danish State Railways; tel: 70 13 14 15; <www.dsb.dk>) and travel to Malmö, then to Helsingborg by train, across the sound to Helsingør, and back to Copenhagen by train.

H

HEALTH AND MEDICAL CARE

Make sure your health insurance covers any illness or accident while travelling. Your travel agent or insurance company will advise you.

In Denmark, treatment and even hospitalisation is free for any tourist taken suddenly ill or involved in an accident. For minor treatments, doctors, dentists and pharmacists will charge on the spot. For EU members, this money will be partly refunded at the local Danish health service office on production of receipts and the European Health Insurance card, obtainable from post offices in the UK.

A Danish pharmacy *(apotek)* is strictly a dispensary. Pharmacies are listed in the phone book under *Apoteker*. Opening hours are 9am–5.30pm and until 1pm on Sat. An all-night service operates at Steno Apotek, Vesterbrogade 69, tel: 33 14 82 66; and at Sønderbro Apotek, Amangerbrog 158, tel: 32 58 01 40.

I need a doctor/dentist.	**Jeg har brug for en læge/tandlæge.**

HOLIDAYS *(fest-/helligdag)*

Though Denmark's banks, offices and major shops close on public holidays, museums, cafés and tourist attractions will mostly be open.

1 January	Nytår	New Year's Day
5 June (half-day)	Grundslovsdag	Constitution Day
24/25/26 December	Christmas	
31 December	New Year's Eve	
Moveable dates:		
Skœrtorsdag	Maundy Thursday	
Langfredag	Good Friday	
Anden påskedag	Easter Monday	
Bededag	General Prayer Day (fourth Friday after Easter)	
Kristi himmelfartsdag	Ascension Day	
Anden pinsedag	Whit Monday	

L

LANGUAGE

English is widely spoken and understood. Danish is perhaps the most difficult northern-European language for relating the written word to speech; it's almost impossible to pronounce simply by reading the words, as many syllables are swallowed rather than spoken. Thus the island of Amager becomes Am-air, with the 'g' disappearing, but in a distinctively Danish way difficult for the visitor to imitate. The letter 'd' becomes something like a 'th', but with the tongue placed behind the lower teeth, not the upper. The letter 'ø' is like the 'u' in English 'nurse', but spoken with the lips far forward. And the letter 'r' is again swallowed.

There are 29 letters in the Danish alphabet including 'æ' (as in egg), 'ø', and 'å' (as in port). They appear after the usual 26 (a point to note when looking up names in phone books and lists).

Days

Monday	**mandag**	Friday	**fredag**
Tuesday	**tirsdag**	Saturday	**lørdag**
Wednesday	**onsdag**	Sunday	**søndag**
Thursday	**torsdag**		

Months

January	**januar**	July	**juli**
February	**februar**	August	**august**
March	**marts**	September	**september**
April	**april**	October	**oktober**
May	**maj**	November	**november**
June	**juni**	December	**december**

Numbers

0	**nul**	10	**ti**	20	**tyve**
1	**en**	11	**elleve**	30	**tredive**
2	**to**	12	**tolv**	40	**fyrre**
3	**tre**	13	**tretten**	50	**halvtreds**
4	**fire**	14	**fjorten**	60	**tres**
5	**fem**	15	**femten**	70	**halvfjerds**
6	**seks**	16	**seksten**	80	**firs**
7	**syv**	17	**sytten**	90	**halvfems**
8	**otte**	18	**atten**	100	**hundrede**
9	**ni**	19	**nitten**	1000	**tusind**

LAUNDRY AND DRY CLEANING *(vask; kemisk rensning)*

The large hotels offer same-day service, but generally not at weekends and holidays – and it's usually expensive. Dry cleaners are listed in the phone book *(Fagbog)* under *Renserier*. Prices in launderettes *(selvbetjeningsvaskeri)* are lower, and these are open until late at night.

When will it be ready?	**Hvornår er det færdigt?**
I must have this for	**Jeg skal bruge det i**
tomorrow morning.	** morgen tidlig.**

LOST PROPERTY *(hittegods)*

The general lost-property office *(hittegodskontor)* is at the police station at Slotsherrensvej 113, Vanløse (tel: 38 74 88 22), Mon, Wed, Fri 9am–2pm, Tues and Thurs 9am–5.30pm. For property lost on trains contact DSB, Reventlowsgade 9, tel: 33 16 21 10, open Mon–Fri 9am–4pm, Thur till 6pm. For missing credit cards: American Express, tel: 70 20 70 97; Diners Club, tel: 70 20 30 77; Access, Eurocard, Eurocheques, MasterCard, JCB and Visa, tel: 44 89 29 29.

M

MEDIA

Newspapers and magazines *(avis; ugeblad)*. You'll have no problem finding English-language newspapers and magazines at newsstands, shops and hotels throughout central Copenhagen. The kiosk at Central Station sells foreign-language publications, and there is a good selection at Magasin du Nord (Kongens Nytorv13) and Illums (Østergade 52–54) department stores. There is also a free monthly English-language booklet, *Copenhagen This Week*, which lists comprehensive information for visitors. The *Copenhagen Post* is a weekly newspaper which prints Danish news in English, also available from kiosks in central Copenhagen. It has a good listings guide.

Have you any English-language newspapers?	**Har De engelsksprogede aviser?**

Radio and TV *(radio; fjernsyn)*. BBC long-wave and world services and European-based American networks can be picked up. Most hotels have satellite TV with stations from the US and Europe.

MONEY MATTERS

Currency. The unit of Danish currency is the kroner, abbreviated kr, or, abroad, DKK (to distinguish it from the Norwegian and Swedish kroner). It is divided into 100 øre. Coins: 25 and 50 øre; 1, 2, 5, 10 and 20 kroner. Banknotes: 50, 100, 200, 500 and 1,000 kroner.

Banks and currency-exchange offices *(bank; vekselkontor)*. Banks and exchange bureaux offer the best exchange rates for foreign cash. You pay a flat commission per transaction at banks, which are open Mon–Fri 9.30am–4pm (until 6pm Thurs), although some at airports and the main railway stations keep longer hours. Outside banking hours, exchange bureaux operate at Central Station, the airport and other locations.

Credit cards and traveller's cheques *(kreditkort; rejsecheck)*. Most institutions will accept payment by most international credit cards. Credit/debit cards can also be used in ATM machines to obtain kroner (cheaper and more convenient than exchanging cash). Traveller's cheques can be cashed at banks, provided you show your passport.

Tax. Danish VAT is called MOMS and is set at 25 percent. It's always included in the bill. For purchases totalling at least 300kr in any one store, foreign visitors can claim a tax refund. In shops displaying the Global Tax-Free Shopping sign; retailers should know the necessary procedures.

Do you accept credit cards? Can you change a traveller's cheque for me?	**Godtager I kreditkort? Kan jeg indløse en rejsecheck?**

O

OPENING HOURS

Banks are open Mon–Fri 9.30am–4pm, Thurs until 6pm. In the provinces, hours fluctuate from town to town.

Post offices are open 9 or 10am–5 or 5.30pm during the week; some post offices are also open on Sat 9am–1pm.

Shops and department stores are generally open Mon–Fri 9am or 10am–5.30pm, 7pm or 8pm. Some are closed on Monday or Tuesday. On Saturday, shops are usually open from 9am–1 or 2pm. Some shops, especially in the tourist areas, stay open for longer hours.

Museums are often closed on Monday and generally open for shorter hours during the winter.

P

POLICE See also EMERGENCIES

State and city police all form part of the national force and are dressed in black uniforms. Some walk their beat through central Copenhagen, but most policemen patrol in dark-blue-and-white or white cars with the word *'politi'* in large letters. You are entitled to stop police cars at any time and request help. Police are courteous and speak English.

Where's the nearest police station?	**Hvor er den nærmeste politi-station?**

POST OFFICES (*postkontor*)

The main post office is at Tietgensgade 35–39 (just behind Tivoli); business hours are Mon–Fri 11am–6pm, Sat 10am–1pm. The post office at Central Station operates longer hours: Mon–Fri 8am–10pm, Sat 9am–4pm, Sun 10am–5pm. There are also many sub-offices around town. All post offices display a red sign with a crown, bugle and crossed arrows in yellow – and a sign saying *Kongelig Post og Telegraf.* When buying postcards from stands and souvenir shops, you can get the appropriate stamps on the spot. Danish postboxes are bright red and stand out cheerfully, as do the postmen – colourful characters in red uniforms riding yellow cycles.

You can pick up poste restante mail at the main post office at Tietgensgade 35–39 (postal address: DK-1500 Copenhagen V); identification is necessary.

PUBLIC TRANSPORT

HT Buses and S-Train. An excellent public-transport system with frequent bus and electrified train (S-tog) service covers not only Copenhagen but its extensive metropolitan area. For bus information, tel: 36 13 14 15 (7am–9.30pm), or consult <www.hur.dk>; for S-train information see <www.dsb.dk>.

Metro. (tel: 33 11 17 00; <www.orestadsselskabet.dk>) Automated trains cover parts of the city on two lines – M1 and M2. They run between 5am and 1am with night services on Friday and Saturday.

Tickets. The Copenhagen metropolitan area is split into seven zones and a ticket allows travel on buses, S-trains and the metro. A basic ticket permits travel within two zones for one hour and costs 19kr (9.50kr for children). A 24-hour ticket costs 110kr (55kr for children) and permits 24 hours of unlimited travel. Discount clip cards *(klippekort)* are available for 10 journeys. A two-zone card costs 115kr (55kr for children). The duration of the validity of tickets and discount clip cards depends on the numbers of zones in which you travel: 2–3 zones – 1 hour; 4–6 zones – 1½ hours; all zones – 2 hours.

How much is a ticket to...?	**Hvad koster en billet to...?**
One ticket to..., please.	**En billet til..., tak.**
Where does this train/ bus go?	**Hvor kører dette tog/ denne bus hen?**

Harbour Bus. (<www.ht.dk>) Runs six times an hour 6am–6pm between the Royal Library on Christians Brygge and the Little Mermaid with stops at Nyhaven and Holmen North.

Taxis. Plenty of taxis cruise the streets of Copenhagen. They are recognisable by a Taxi or *Taxa* sign, and vacant cabs display the word *fri* (free). Tipping is not necessary, but round the sum up if you are impressed by the service. The basic fare is 19kr plus 10kr per km between 7am–4pm, 11kr 4pm–7am, 13kr Fri–Sat 11pm–7am and 11kr on Sunday and national holidays. Most drivers accept credit cards.

Trains *(tog)*. A comprehensive and generally punctual network, which covers the entire country, operates from Copenhagen Central Station.

R

RELIGION

The Danish Church is Protestant (Danish Lutheran Evangelical), and 92 percent of Danes are members. Services in English are held at:

Church of England. St Alban's Anglican Episcopalian Church, Churchillparken, Langelinie. Sunday morning services, Holy Communion 9am and Family Eucharist 10.30am; Wednesday Holy Communion 10.30am (tel: 39 62 77 36; <www.st-albans.dk>).

Roman Catholic. Sacrament's Church (Sakramentskirken), Nørrebrogade 27. Services in English Sunday 6pm and Wednesday 5pm. (tel: 35 35 68 25; <www.sakramentskirken.dk>).

Jewish services. Great Synagogue, Krystalgade 12 (tel: 33 12 88 68).

T

TELEPHONES *(telefon)*

The country code for Denmark is 45. The country code for Great Britain is 44, the USA and Canada 1, Australia 61, New Zealand 64, the Republic of Ireland 353 and South Africa 27. Phone boxes generally take prepaid telephone cards that can be purchased from shops and kiosks.

TIME ZONES

Denmark operates on Central European Time (GMT + 1). In summer, the clock is put one hour ahead (GMT + 2). The time differences are:

New York	London	**Copenhagen**	Jo'burg	Sydney
7am	noon	**1pm**	1pm	9pm

TIPPING

In general you don't give tips unless special services have been rendered. Hotel and restaurant bills always include service. Railway porters charge fixed prices, and there is no need to tip hairdressers or taxi drivers. You may like to leave the odd kroner tip for use of facilities in toilets.

TOILETS

Facilities are usually indicated by a pictograph; alternatively they are marked WC, *Toiletter*, *Damer/Herrer* (Ladies/Gentlemen), or just D/H. There is no charge unless you see it clearly marked otherwise.

TOURIST INFORMATION *(turistinformation)*

In Copenhagen the main place to go is the Copenhagen Tourist Information Office, 4a Vesterbrogade, across from Central Station and just outside Tivoli (open May–June Mon–Sat 9am–6pm, closed Sun; July–Aug Mon–Sat 9am–8pm, Sun 10am–6pm; Sept–Apr Mon–Sat 9am–4pm; tel: 70 22 24 42; fax: 70 22 24 52; <www.visitcopenhagen. com>). Besides offering a comprehensive array of tourist information, posters and postcards, the office also offers personal assistance with booking sightseeing tours and hotel and private accommodation. **Copenhagen Card.** The Tourist Information Office is also one of the many places where you may purchase the Copenhagen Card. The City Card lasts for 24 or 72 hours and gives free or reduced admission to more than 60 popular museums and sights in the city. It also grants free travel on buses, S-trains, Metro and the harbour bus throughout the region as well as discounts on car hire and Scandlines ferry routes between Denmark and Sweden. The cost for 24 hours is 199kr (children 10–15 years 129kr), for 72 hours 429kr (children 10–15 years 249kr). With these cards two children under 10 years may accompany each adult free of charge.

All Danish cities and most small towns have their own Tourist Information Office marked by a large letter 'i' on a green background.
UK: Danish Tourist Board, 55 Sloane Street, London SW1X 9SY; tel: 020 7259 5959; fax 020 7259 5955; e-mail <dtb.london@dt.dk>.
US: Danish Tourist Board, 655 Third Avenue, 18th floor, New York, NY 10017; tel: (212) 885-9700; fax (212) 885-9726.

| Where's the Tourist Office? | **Hvor ligger turistbureauet?** |

W

WEBSITES

The Danish Tourist Board has comprehensive information at <www.visitdenmark.com>; Wonderful Copenhagen has a wealth of information at <www.woco.dk>; and *Copenhagen This Week* carries details of what's on each month at <www.ctw.dk>. Other websites are listed alongside the individual entries throughout Travel Tips.

Y

YOUTH HOSTELS *(vandrerhjem)*

There are 12 city youth hostels and student hotels. Youth hostels require an International Youth Hostel Association membership card or a guest card from Danmarks Vandrerhjem (Denmark's Youth Hostels), Vesterbrogade 39, DK-1620 Copenhagen V; tel: 31 31 36 12; fax 31 31 36 26; <www.danhostel.dk>. Open Mon–Thurs 9am–4pm, Fri until 3pm.

At a student hotel *(ungdomsherberg)*, restrictions on night-time closing and other practices are more relaxed.

Recommended Hotels

Most of Copenhagen's hotels are clustered near the city's main sights – Rådhuspladsen, Tivoli Gardens, the University Quarter and the lively shopping area along Strøget.

The following hotels are listed alphabetically, area by area. The price categories are based on the cost per night of a double room with bath or shower (unless indicated otherwise) in the high season, including service charge, VAT (MOMS) and breakfast. These rates can be as much as 50 percent lower at other times of the year.

It is always advisable to reserve ahead of your stay. The city is at its busiest in the summer months (June–August), but conferences ensure that hotels are kept busy throughout the year.

Check out the excellent overview on <www.visitcopenhagen.dk>, where you can also make bookings.

€€€€	over 2,000kr
€€€	1,500–2,000kr
€€	1,000–1,500kr
€	under 1,000kr

AROUND RADHUSPLADSEN

Hotel Alexandra €€ *H.C. Andersens Boulevard 8, DK-1553 Copenhagen V, tel: 33 74 44 44, fax: 33 74 44 88, <www.hotel-alexandra.dk>.* A lovely old hotel in a building originating from 1880, situated almost next door to Rådhuspladsen. The hotel is pleasantly decorated, with light, airy rooms and excellent facilities. 61 rooms.

Ascot Hotel €€ *Studiestræde 61, DK-1554 Copenhagen V, tel: 33 12 60 00, fax: 33 14 60 40, <www.ascot-hotel.dk>.* Set in a distinguished old bathhouse building a few steps from City Hall. Pleasantly decorated with a mixture of antiques and modern furniture. 155 rooms.

Hotel Astoria €€ *Banegårdspladsen 4, DK-1570 Copenhagen V, tel: 33 42 99 00, fax: 33 42 99 99, <www.astoriahotelcopenhagen. dk>*. Dating from 1936, its bizarre façade is an excellent architectural example of Cubist style. The rooms have been updated to meet modern tastes, some have as many as five beds and are particularly suitable for families. 94 rooms.

Carlton Hotel Guldsmeden €€ *Vesterbrogade 66, DK-1620 Copenhagen V, tel: 33 22 15 00, fax: 33 22 15 15, <www.hotel guldsmeden.dk>*. A charming three-star hotel located in the lively Vesterbro neighbourhood, close to many small, hip shops and cafes. Tasty organic breakfast with breads from a nearby gourmet bakery. 64 rooms.

Clarion Collection Hotel Mayfair €€ *Helgolandsgade 3, DK-1653 Copenhagen V, tel: 70 12 17 00, fax: 33 23 96 86, <www. choicehotels.dk>*. An early 20th-century hotel that has recently been refurbished. It offers a cosy atmosphere coupled with a very high standard of personal service. 106 rooms.

Hotel Danmark €€ *Vester Voldgade 89, DK-1552 Copenhagen V, tel: 33 11 48 06, fax: 33 14 36 30, <www.hotel-danmark.dk>*. Adjacent to Rådhuspladsen and close to Strøget. Modern bright building with rooms tastefully furnished in subdued Scandinavian style. Underground parking. 88 rooms.

DGI-Byen €€ *Tietgensgade 65, DK-1704 Copenhagen V, tel: 33 29 80 50, <www.dgi-byen.dk>*. Situated very close to Central Station and Tivoli, this new hotel is sleek Danish design at its best. Some rooms with balconies. Conference facilities. Attached to the hotel is the Vandkulturhuset, Copenhagen's state-of-the-art swimming complex, athletics centre and spa. 104 rooms.

First Hotel Vesterbro €€€€ *Vesterbrogade 23–29, DK-1620 Copenhagen V, tel: 33 78 80 00, fax: 33 78 80 80, <www.firsthotels. com>*. This modern four-star hotel has a great location in trendy Vesterbro. Modern rooms, excellent service, good restaurant and bar, and just a five-minute walk from Tivoli and Rådhuspladsen. 403 rooms.

Grand Hotel €€€ *Vesterbrogade 9A, DK-1620 Copenhagen V, tel: 33 27 69 00, fax: 33 27 69 01, <www.grandhotel.dk>.* An enticing façade, dating from 1890, fronts a four-star hotel that has been carefully modernised in a manner that preserves much of its original character. Tastefully decorated. 161 rooms.

IBIS Copenhagen Crown Hotel € *Vesterbrogade 41, DK-1620 Copenhagen V, tel: 33 21 21 66, fax: 33 21 00 66, <www.accor hotels.com>.* The entrance is in a quiet courtyard just off this busy street. Pleasant rooms, and just a few minutes' walk from Rådhuspladsen. 80 rooms.

Imperial Hotel €€€–€€€€ *Vester Farimagsgade 9, DK-1606 Copenhagen V, tel: 33 12 80 00, fax: 33 12 80 03, <www.imperial hotel.dk>.* Good location next to Vesterport Station, a few minutes' walk from Rådhuspladsen and Tivoli Gardens. Modern, well-appointed, elegant rooms, fine restaurants and on-site parking. 163 rooms.

Hotel Kong Frederik €€ *Vester Voldgade 25, DK-1552 Copenhagen V, tel: 33 12 59 02, fax: 33 93 59 01, <www.remmen.dk>.* Although named in 1898, its history as hotel and inn dates back to the 14th century. Situated close to Rådhuspladsen and Tivoli. A recent renovation has retained its classical English atmosphere. 110 rooms.

Marriott €€€ *Kalvebod Brygge, DK-1560 Copenhagen V, tel: 88 33 99 00, fax: 88 33 99 99, <www.marriott.com/cphdk>.* A luxury glass and concrete block offers all that one expects from Marriott hotels. Waterside rooms overlook the inner harbour. 395 rooms.

Norlandia Mercure Hotel €€ *Vester Farimagsgade 17, DK-1606 Copenhagen V, tel: 33 12 57 11, fax: 33 12 57 17, <www.norlandia hotels.dk>.* Just behind Vesterport Station, this is a pleasant tourist-class hotel, with an outdoor tennis court available to guests for a small fee. 109 rooms.

Norlandia Richmond Hotel €€ *Vester Farimagsgade 33, DK-1606 Copenhagen V, tel: 33 12 33 66, fax: 33 12 97 17, <www. norlandiahotels.dk>.* Also close to Vesterport Station, this is slightly more upmarket than its sister hotel, the Mercure. Sound-proof windows. Newly renovated. 127 rooms.

Norlandia Star Hotel € *Colbjørnsensgade 13, DK-1652 Copenhagen V, tel: 33 22 11 00, fax: 33 21 21 86, <www.norlandiahotels.dk>.* Situated in the cluster of streets on the other side of Central Station from Tivoli. Well-appointed rooms and an inviting Jacuzzi. Newly renovated.134 rooms.

Palace Hotel €€€€ *Rådhuspladsen 57, DK-1550 Copenhagen V, tel: 33 14 40 50, fax: 33 14 52 79, <www.palace-hotel.dk>.* An imposing historical landmark on Rådhuspladsen, the Palace has been carefully renovated and modernised over the years to the highest standards. Forty ambassador-class rooms overlook Rådhuspladsen and Tivoli Gardens. 162 rooms.

Radisson SAS Royal €€€€ *Hammerichsgade 1, DK-1611 Copenhagen V, tel: 33 42 60 00, fax: 33 42 61 00, <www.radissonsas.com>.* Dating from 1960, this modern 20-storey hotel offers a panoramic view of Tivoli Gardens and the city. Centrally located and just a short walk from Rådhuspladsen, Strøget and the University Quarter. Rooms are in modern Danish design. There is a rooftop restaurant, sauna and private parking. 265 rooms.

Scandic Webers €€€ *Vesterbrogade 11B, DK-1620 Copenhagen V, tel: 33 31 44 32, fax: 33 31 14 41, <www.scandic-hotels.com/webers>.* Newly opened after thorough renovation. Great breakfast, trendy bar, peaceful courtyard. 152 rooms.

Sofitel Plaza Copenhagen €€€ *Bernstorffsgade 4, DK-1577 Copenhagen V, tel: 33 14 92 62, fax: 33 93 93 62, <www.accorhotels.com>.* Commissioned by Frederik VIII in 1913, this hotel has beautifully appointed rooms and lovely decoration throughout. The attractive Library Bar has been voted one of the five best bars in the world by *Forbes Magazine*. Delicious buffet breakfast. 93 rooms.

The Square €€ *Rådhuspladsen 14, DK-1550 Copenhagen V, tel: 33 38 12 00, fax: 33 38 12 01, <www.thesquare.dk>.* In the heart of

Rådhuspladsen, this new, sleek hotel offers much for its three stars. Several grades of rooms. Rooftop breakfast room with fine views. 192 rooms (46 singles).

AROUND KONGENS NYTORV

Hotel d'Angleterre €€€€ *Kongens Nytorv 34, DK-1050 Copenhagen K, tel: 33 12 00 95, fax: 33 12 11 18, <www.rem men.dk>*. Established more than 250 years ago, this hotel offers its guests a certain old-fashioned grandness. With a superb location overlooking Kongens Nytorv, it is often named the best hotel in Denmark, though it can sometimes seem a bit tired around the edges. 123 rooms.

Copenhagen Strand €€€ *Havnegade 37, DK-1058 Copenhagen K, tel: 33 48 99 00, fax: 33 48 99 01, <www.copenhagenstrand. dk>*. Opened in 2000, this ultra-modern hotel is in a converted warehouse dating from 1869. Situated on a side street just off Nyhavn, close to Kongens Nytorv. 174 rooms.

Hotel Opera €€ *Todenskjoldsgade 15, DK-1055 Copenhagen K, tel: 33 47 83 00, fax: 33 47 83 01, <www.operahotelcopenhagen. dk>*. Located close to the Royal Theatre at Kongens Nytorv. Dating from 1869, a recent renovation introduced 'Olde England' decor. 91 rooms.

NYHAVN AND BEYOND

Adina Apartment Hotel Copenhagen €€€ *Amerikaplads 7, DK-2100 Copenhagen Ø, tel: 39 63 10 00, fax: 88 19 36 99, <www. adina.dk>*. Fully-equipped four-star hotel apartments with conference facilities, fitness center, swimming pool and restaurant. Close to the Little Mermaid. 126 rooms.

Comfort Hotel Esplanaden €–€€ *Bredgade 78, DK-1260 Copenhagen K, tel: 33 48 10 00, fax: 33 48 10 66, <www.choice hotels.dk>*. Located between Amalienborg and the Little Mermaid in the 250-year old Frederiksstad quarter. A recently renovated economy hotel, part of the Choice chain, with clean pleasant rooms. 117 rooms, all non-smoking.

Copenhagen Admiral Hotel €€€ *Tolbodgade 24–28, DK-1253 Copenhagen K, tel: 33 74 14 14, fax: 33 74 14 16, <www.admiral hotel.dk>*. Standing beside the harbour, the hotel was formerly a granary constructed in 1787. Comfortably converted, it has retained the 200-year-old Pomeranian pine wooden beams in the rooms. Features its own restaurant, nightclub and sauna. 366 rooms.

Front €€ *Sankt Annæ Plads 21, DK-1250 Copenhagen K, tel: 33 37 06 56, fax: 33 37 06 30, <www.front.dk>*. This modern boutique hotel is located on the harbour front adjacent to Amalienborg Palace and close to Nyhavn. Sleek, well-equipped rooms. 134 rooms.

71 Nyhavn Hotel €€€ *Nyhavn 71, DK-1051 Copenhagen K, tel: 33 43 62 00, fax: 33 43 62 01, <www.71nyhavnhotel.com>*. Delightfully located at the foot of Nyhavn in a well-renovated and carefully restored warehouse. A modern hotel with rather small rooms, a rustic atmosphere and great views over the harbour. 150 rooms.

Phoenix Copenhagen €€€ *Bredgade 37, DK-1260 Copenhagen K, tel: 33 95 95 00, fax: 33 33 98 33, <www.phoenixcopenhagen. com>*. An elegant de-luxe hotel close to the Royal Palace and Kongens Nytorv. All rooms and suites are air-conditioned and furnished elegantly in the French Louis XVI style. 213 rooms.

UNIVERSITY QUARTER AND PARKS

Hotel Christian IV €€ *Dronningens Tværgade 45, DK-1302 Copenhagen K, tel: 33 32 10 44, fax: 33 32 07 06, <www.hotel christianiv.dk>*. A small pleasing hotel located right by the lovely King's Garden. Rooms are neat and bright, and fitted with modern Danish furniture. Quiet neighbourhood. 42 rooms.

Hotel Fox €€ *Jarmers Plads 3, DK-1551 Copenhagen V, tel: 33 13 30 00, fax: 33 14 30 33, <www.hotelfox.dk>*. A truly unique hotel that redefines the term 'design hotel'. Each room is designed differently by one of 21 young European artists. Some cool, some very strange. Located in the Latin Quarter close to cult hang-outs. 61 rooms.

Hotel Kong Arthur €€€ *Nørre Søgade 11, DK-1370 Copenhagen V, tel: 33 11 12 12, fax: 33 32 61 30, <www.kongarthur.dk>.* Established in 1882, and situated beside Peblinge Lake, this hotel has retained much of its original charm. A popular choice with both Danish and foreign visitors; it has a friendly and thoroughly Danish atmosphere. 107 rooms.

Ibsens Hotel €€ *Vendersgade 23, DK-1363 Copenhagen K, tel: 33 13 19 13, fax: 33 13 19 16, <www.ibsenshotel.dk>.* Close to Nørreport Station and the city centre, this comfortable hotel is nothing fancy, but has some great perks, like free wireless internet in all rooms, and good tapas and sushi restaurants next door. 118 rooms.

Skt Petri €€€–€€€€ *Krystalgade 22, DK-1172 Copenhagen K, tel: 33 45 91 00, fax: 33 45 91 10, <www.hotelsktpetri.com>.* The only Scandinavian hotel to make *Condé Nast Traveler's* '100 Best New Hotels' list in 2005. Five stars for hipness, this design hotel shows great attention to detail, right down to the electronica music its staff commissions and pipes into the lifts. Absolutely the best breakfast buffet in the city. 27 suites. 268 rooms.

OUTLYING AREAS

Hilton Copenhagen Airport €€€ *Ellehammersvej 20, DK-2770 Copenhagen, tel: 32 50 15 01, fax: 32 52 85 28, <www.hilton.dk>.* Copenhagen's largest rooms, five star luxury and a lobby filled with famous Arne Jacobsen chairs usually holding famous celebrities. Can't get closer to the airport – this is part of Terminal 3. 382 rooms.

Radisson SAS Scandinavia Hotel €€€ *Amager Boulevard 70, DK-2300 Copenhagen S, tel: 33 96 50 00, fax: 33 96 55 00, <www. radissonsas.com>.* A 25-storey building that dominates the skyline 1km (⅔ mile) from Tivoli Gardens across the water on Amager. Rooms furnished in standard, Scandinavian or Oriental decor, most having fine views. Convenient for the airport. 542 rooms.

Recommended Restaurants

With more than 2,000 restaurants, cafés, bars and snack bars, many of them serving ethnic cuisine, Copenhagen is something of a gourmet's paradise. This particularly applies to the ten establishments that were awarded Michelin stars in 2006. Whether you fancy a quick coffee and *wienerbrød* or a five-course feast, you'll have plenty of places to choose from. There are nearly 40 eating establishments inside Tivoli Gardens alone. For *frokost* (lunch), cafés serve a selection of hot dishes and *smørrebrød* (open sandwiches) at reasonable prices. *Middag* (dinner) can be as light or as heavy as you like, and many places offer traditional *kolde bord* (cold table), where you can eat as much as you wish for a set charge.

The restaurants below represent a cross-section of what is available. Prices are based on the cost of a meal for two people, including tax but excluding drinks. Note that the high import duty on wine can add considerably to the final bill. For an up-to-date listing of restaurants, consult the free monthly *Copenhagen This Week (see page 120).*

€€€€€	over 1,000kr
€€€€	between 500–1,000kr
€€€	between 250–500kr
€€	between 100–250kr
€	below 100kr

AROUND RADHUSPLADSEN

A Hereford Beefstouw €€€ *by Tivoli, Vesterbrogade 3, DK-1620 Copenhagen V, tel: 33 12 74 41, fax: 33 12 18 24, <www.a-h-b.dk>.* Juicy steaks cooked to order and tasty seafood dishes. A restaurant chain with a difference; a percentage of the profits are invested in the quality art that adorns the restaurants. Open daily for lunch and dinner.

Café Ultimo €€€ *Tivoli, Vesterbrogade 3, DK-1630 Copenhagen V, tel: 33 75 07 51, <www.cafeultimotivoli.dk>*. Inspired Italian cuisine served in what was once a dance hall, then a hippodrome. Open daily noon–10pm.

Carlton €€ *Halmtorvet 14, DK-1700 Copenhagen V, tel: 33 29 90 90, <www.carltonkbhv.dk>*. Trendy restaurant and café located in an up-and-coming area west of Central Station. Delightful atmosphere, limited menu, great outdoor space. Vegetarian brunch is served till 3pm. Open Monday–Friday 10am–midnight, Saturday–Sunday till 2am.

Copenhagen Corner €€€ *Rådhuspladsen, Vesterbrogade 1A, DK-1620 Copenhagen V, tel: 33 91 45 45, fax: 33 91 04 04, <www.remmen.dk>*. Excellent French/Danish cuisine in a brightly decorated restaurant overlooking City Hall. Open daily from 11.30am until 11pm.

Formel B €€€€€ *Vesterbrogade 182, DK-1800 Frederiksberg C, tel: 33 25 10 66, <www.formel-b.dk>*. Impeccable gastronomic experience. One Michelin star. Classical French cooking honed with Danish raw materials inspired by the modern European kitchen. Open Monday–Saturday 6–10pm.

India Palace €€ *H.C. Andersens Boulevard 13, DK-1553 Copenhagen V, tel: 33 91 44 08*. A restaurant serving authentic Indian cuisine in pleasant surroundings just a short step from Rådhuspladsen. The India Palace's delicious all-you-can-eat lunch and dinner buffets provide excellent value. A la carte dishes also available. Open daily 11am–midnight.

Mongolian Barbecue €€ *Stormgade 35, DK-1555 Copenhagen V, Copenhagen, tel: 33 14 64 66*. This popular restaurant provides an excellent-value Mongolian buffet with as much as you can eat for a set price. Open daily 4pm–midnight.

Passagens Spisehus €€€ *Vesterbrogade 42, DK-1620, Copenhagen V, tel: 33 22 47 57*. The place for Nordic food. Starters include dried cod and Lapland carpaccio; main courses feature wild musk from Greenland, reindeer and moose. Affordable set meals in somewhat stark decor. Decent wines. Open every day for lunch and dinner.

Restaurant Balkonen Tivoli €€€–€€€€ *Tivoli, Vesterbrogade 3, DK-1630 Copenhagen V, tel: 33 75 07 27, fax: 33 75 07 17, <www.balkonen.dk>*. One of the many restaurants in Tivoli, this one is located on a prominent balcony overlooking the gardens. Varied menu with seafood, a carvery and a popular salad bar. Open daily for lunch and dinner in the summer.

Rio Bravo €€ *Vester Voldgade 86, DK-1552 Copenhagen V, tel: 33 11 75 87, fax: 33 13 53 48, <www.riobravo.dk>*. A no-nonsense cowboy-style steak house, where even the seats at the bar are saddles. A popular restaurant and a firm favourite with Copenhagen's late-night revellers. Open Monday–Saturday 11.30am–4am, Sunday from 5pm.

STRØGET AND BEYOND

Brasserie Ego €€€€ *Hovedvagtsgade 2, DK-1103 Copenhagen K, tel: 33 12 79 71, fax: 33 91 63 19, <www.egocph.dk>*. Classic French food and Danish lunches, carefully prepared and pleasingly presented. Open for lunch and dinner Tuesday–Saturday.

Café à Porta €€€ *Kongens Nytorv 17, DK-1050 Copenhagen K, tel: 33 11 05 00, fax: 33 11 05 52, <www.cafeaporta.dk>*. One of the city's oldest and most popular cafés, dating from 1788. An ideal stop for a meal or a drink, situated between the shopping area of Strøget and Nyhavn. French menu has slowly given way to more local dishes. Café open all day.

Caféen i Nikolaj €–€€ *Nikolaj Plads 12, DK-1067 Copenhagen K, tel: 70 26 64 64*. In a wing of the Nikolaj Church, alongside the Copenhagen Contemporary Art Centre, this is a popular spot with the locals. A good spot for *frokost* (lunch). Open Monday–Saturday 11.30am–5pm.

Café Sorgenfri € *Brolæggerstræde 8, DK-1211 Copenhagen K, tel: 33 11 58 80.* Central location just south of Strøget, this Danish diner serves *smørrebrød* and classic dishes below ground level. Good reputation. Open daily 10am–11pm.

Kanal-Caféen €–€€ *Frederiksholms Kanal 18, DK-1220 Copenhagen K, tel: 33 11 57 70.* Enjoy a *smørrebrød* in a maritime atmosphere at this Danish diner. Herring from the fishing grounds off Bornholm. Open Monday–Friday 11.30am–7pm, Saturday 10.30am–4pm.

Københavner Caféen €€ *Badstuestræde 10, DK-1209 Copenhagen K, tel: 33 32 80 81.* A delightful restaurant just off Strøget, heading south in the direction of Gammel Strand. Particularly recommended for its Danish cold table and the daily Copenhagen Plate offering seven items for a very reasonable set price. Open daily 11.30am–11pm.

Kommandanten €€€€–€€€€€ *Ny Adelgade 7, DK-1104 Copenhagen K, tel: 33 12 09 90, fax: 33 93 12 23, <www.kommand anten.com>.* Situated in a 1698 townhouse decorated by the floral artist and interior designer, Tage Andersen. This Michelin-starred restaurant is both a visual and culinary experience. Open Monday–Saturday for dinner.

Kong Hans Kælder €€€€–€€€€€ *Vingaardsstræde 6, DK-1070 Copenhagen K, tel: 33 11 68 68, fax: 33 32 67 68, <www.konghans.dk>.* Located in the oldest building in Copenhagen, its Gothic arches giving it a medieval flavour. The restaurant serves classical French cuisine and very fine wines, and has its own salmon smokehouse. One Michelin star. Open Monday–Saturday for dinner.

Krogs Fiskerestaurant €€€€–€€€€€ *Gammel Strand 38, DK-1202 Copenhagen K, tel: 33 15 89 15, fax: 33 15 83 19, <www.krogs.dk>.* In an 18th-century building with early-20th-century decor, this restaurant is justly renowned for its excellent fish dishes. Reservations are recommended. Kitchen open Monday–Saturday from 6pm–midnight.

Pierre André Fransk Restaurant €€€€ *Ny Østergade 21, DK-1101 Copenhagen K, tel: 33 16 17 19, fax: 33 16 17 72, <www.pierreandre.dk>.* Opened in early 1996, this 35-seat restaurant has always had a reputation for culinary excellence. The cuisine is classic modern French/Italian and the menu changes every two months. Exclusive wine list. Open Monday–Saturday for dinner.

Restaurant L'Alsace €€€–€€€€ *Ny Østergade 9/Pistolstræde, DK-1101, Copenhagen K, tel: 33 14 57 43, fax: 33 12 80 21, <www.alsace.dk>.* Situated in a charming courtyard surrounded by 17th-century buildings. An interesting and diverse menu, with specialities such as Iberian ham, oysters, caviar and other seafood. Open Monday–Saturday for lunch and dinner.

Restaurant Bali €€–€€€ *Kongens Nytorv 19, DK-1050 Copenhagen K, tel: 33 11 08 08.* Located on the corner of Kongens Nytorv, this restaurant has a tropical feel. Specialises in Indonesian cuisine, including *rijstaffel*, a lavish buffet served with steamed white rice, and offers a selection of lovely, delicately spiced meat and vegetable dishes. Open daily noon–midnight.

RizRaz € *Kompagnistræde 20, DK-1208 Copenhagen K, tel: 33 15 05 75, fax: 33 12 11 49, <www.rizraz.dk>. Also at Kanikkestræde 19.* RizRaz does a splendid Mediterranean vegetarian buffet at low prices. Heaps of tasty food for budget travellers. Open daily 11.30am–midnight.

Slotskælderen hos Gitte Kik €–€€ *Fortunstræde 4, DK-1065 Copenhagen K, tel: 33 11 15 37.* Come here for delightful traditional fare such as *smørrebrød*, served in a cosy basement. Open Tuesday–Saturday 10am–5pm.

NYHAVN AND BEYOND

Els €€€–€€€€ *Store Strandstræde 3, DK-1255 Copenhagen K, tel: 33 14 13 41, fax: 33 91 07 00, <www.restaurant-els.dk>.* The elegant 19th-century decor of this delightful restaurant close to Kongens Nytorv complements the stylish cuisine. Fish is a speciality, and the menu changes every day. Reservations are strongly advised. Open daily for lunch and dinner.

Ergo €€€ *Gothersgade 35, DK-1264 Copenhagen K, tel: 45 85 35 35, <www.er-go.dk>*. A high-quality seasonal menu, wonderfully prepared and at surprisingly low prices. Open for dinner Monday–Saturday.

Fyrskibet €€€ *Nyhavn 61, DK-1051 Copenhagen K, tel: 33 11 19 33*. For something a bit different, dine aboard this lighthouse ship berthed at the foot of Nyhavn. Drinks and snacks on the deck; meals in a glass-enclosed cabin. Fish a speciality. Open Monday–Saturday 10.30am–11pm.

Ida Davidsen €€ *Store Kongensgade 70, DK-1264 Copenhagen K, tel: 33 91 36 55*. Family-run concern in Frederiksstaden serving a delectable selection of *smørrebrød*, with a choice of differently flavoured *akvavit* (Danish schnapps) to accompany it. Traditional decor. Arrive in good time to secure a table for lunch. Highly recommended. Open Monday–Friday 10am–4pm.

Lumskebugten €€€–€€€€ *Esplanaden 21, DK-1263 Copenhagen K, tel: 33 15 60 29, fax: 33 32 87 18, <www.lumskebugten.dk>*. A small and exclusive restaurant by Churchill Park near the Little Mermaid statue. Fine food, fine wine. It is also runs the Royal Barge moored nearby. Reservations are essential. Open Monday– Friday for lunch and dinner, Saturday dinner.

Nyhavns Færgekro €€ *Nyhavn 5, DK-1051 Copenhagen K, tel: 33 15 15 88, fax: 33 15 18 68, <www.nyhavnsfaergekro.dk>*. An unpretentious restaurant serving particularly good traditional food. It's renowned for its herring buffet. Wonderful location alongside Nyhavn; you can choose to sit inside or outside depending on the weather. Open daily 9am–1am.

Pastis €€€ *Gothersgade 52, DK-1264 Copenhagen K, tel: 33 93 44 11*. A new French brasserie with excellent traditional cooking at good prices. Open Monday–Saturday 11am–10.30pm.

Restaurant Rasmus Oubæk €€€–€€€€ *Store Kongensgade 52, DK-1264 Copenhagen K, tel: 33 32 32 09, <www.rasmus oubaek.dk>*. An excellent French brasserie – serving hearty soups, steaks, pies full of flavour – and from one of Copenhagen's most honoured chefs. Open Monday–Friday for lunch and Wednesday– Friday for dinner.

Le Sommelier €€€ *Bredgade 63-65, DK-1260 Copenhagen K, tel: 33 11 45 15, 33 11 59 79, <www.lesommelier.dk>*. French in name and French in style, with a large bar and dining area. Forty wines by the glass and 1,400 in the cellar. Open Monday–Friday for lunch and dinner, Saturday and Sunday for dinner only.

UNIVERSITY QUARTER AND PARKS

Ankara € *Krystalgade 8, DK-1172 Copenhagen K, tel: 33 15 19 15, <www.restaurant-ankara.dk>*. Extensive Turkish buffet modi- fied to suit the Danish palate. Inexpensive wines and coffees. A belly dancer provides entertainment. Open Monday–Saturday 11am–midnight, Sunday 2pm–midnight.

Café Ketchup €€€ *Pilestræde 19, DK-1112 Copenhagen K; Tel; 33 32 30 30, fax: 33 32 30 95, <www.cafeketchup.dk>*. Inventive fusion cuisine – Asian, Danish, French – served in a modern café at the front or in the restaurant behind and below. DJ on Friday and Saturday. Open Monday–Thursday noon–midnight, Friday and Saturday till 4am. Also in Tivoli.

Café & Ølhalle 1892 €–€€ *Rømersgade 22, DK-2200 Copenhagen N, tel: 33 93 25 75*. This 'Café and Beer Hall' is part of Arbejder- museet (the workers' museum). Original turn-of-the-20th-century atmosphere. Real Danish fare. Open daily 11.30am–4pm.

Café Sommersko €–€€ *Kronprinsensgade 6, DK-1114 Copen- hagen K, tel: 33 14 81 89, fax: 33 32 06 63, <www.sommersko.dk>*. Just off Strøget, this is a lively Danish/French café. Varied menu; numerous foreign beers. Kitchen open Monday–Saturday 9am–11pm, Sunday 10am–10pm.

Den Grønne Kælder €–€€ *Pilestræde 48, DK-1112 Copenhagen K, tel: 33 93 01 40*. Excellent place for a vegetarian lunch or dinner. Art decorates the walls and jazz plays in the backgound. Open Monday–Saturday 11am–10pm.

Det Lille Apotek €€–€€€ *Store Kannikestræde 15, DK-1169 Copenhagen K, tel: 33 12 56 06, <www.det-lille-apotek.dk>*. Just a short walk from the Round Tower, 'The Little Pharmacy' is Copenhagen's oldest restaurant. Hans Christian Andersen is said to have dined here; today it's popular with students. Delicious Danish food – try the lunch plate selection for two. Open for lunch Monday–Saturday 11.30am–5pm, dinner 5.30–10pm (Saturday till 11pm); Sunday noon–10pm.

Govindas Vegetar Restaurant €–€€ *Nørre Farimagsgade 82, DK-1364 Copenhagen K, tel: 33 33 74 44, <www.govindas.dk>*. A small unpretentious vegetarian restaurant close to the Botanisk Have. Open Monday–Friday noon–9pm, Saturday 1–7pm.

Kiin Kiin €€€€€ *Guldbergsgade 21, DK-2200 Copenhagen N, tel: 35 35 75 55, fax: 35 35 75 59, <www.kiin.dk>*. 'Eat Eat' in Thai, this authentic, 'updated' Thai restaurant on trendy Sankt Hans Square in Nørrebro has earned the highest reviews in the Danish media – for good reason. The signature dish is shrimp soup ginseng. Open Monday–Saturday for dinner.

Peder Oxe €€–€€€ *Gråbrødretorv 11, DK-1154 Copenhagen K, tel: 33 11 00 77*. Danish and French cuisine in a row of fine restaurants on this attractive square. Outdoor seating, great salad bar, good wine list. Open daily 11.30am–1am.

Restaurant Godt €€€€ *Gothersgade 38, DK-1123 Copenhagen K, tel: 33 15 21 22, <www.restaurant-godt.dk>*. *Godt* means good, which is an understatement for this small, family-run 20-seat restaurant. The cuisine is European with one daily four-course menu and a mainly French, though expanding, wine list. One Michelin star and reservations required. Open Tuesday–Saturday for dinner.

Restaurant Premisse €€€€€ *Dronningens Tværgade 2, DK-1302 Copenhagen K, tel: 33 11 11 45, <www.premisse.dk>*. This restaurant is in a cellar in one of the city's old palaces, a few minutes walk from Rosenborg Slot and the King's Garden. It's run by two chefs who built their reputation at a previous restaurant in the city and the food is well presented and delicious. Open for lunch on weekdays, and Monday–Saturday 6pm–midnight.

Restaurationen €€€€€ *Møntergade 19, DK-1116 Copenhagen K, tel: 33 14 94 95, <www.restaurationen.com>*. A charismatic restaurant close to the Round Tower, very much reflecting the personalities of the owners, Bo and Lisbeth Jacobsen. One fixed-price menu, featuring seasonal produce, which is changed weekly. Open Tuesday–Saturday for dinner; closed July. One Michelin star.

Sankt Gertruds Kloster €€€ *Hauser Plads 32, DK-1127 Copenhagen K, tel: 33 14 66 30, <www.sanktgertrudskloster.dk>*. The vault of a 14th-century monastery is the setting for this restaurant offering specialities from around the world and a wine cellar of more than 39,000 bottles. Reservations are advised. Open daily for dinner.

CHRISTIANSHAVN AND HOLMEN

Era Ora €€€€–€€€€€ *Overgaden Neden Vandet 33B, DK-1414 Copenhagen K, Copenhagen, tel: 32 54 06 93, <www.era-ora.dk>*. Opened in 1983, this restaurant offers Italian cuisine presented innovatively. The most expensive of the three set menus features antipasti, pasta, meat or fish, cheese and then a dessert. One Michelin star. Open Monday–Saturday for dinner.

Restaurant Viva €€€€ *Langebro Kaj 570, DK-1411 Copenhagen K, tel: 27 25 05 05, <www.restaurantviva.dk>*. Based inside a ship moored in the harbour by Langebro, this seafood restaurant seats 70 inside and another 50 on the sun deck in the summer. Plenty of shellfish specialities, stylish decor and the sensation of being on board a ship when a passing speedboat raises waves. Open every day for lunch and dinner.

INDEX